The Bible Speaks
to Me About
My Witness

The Bible Speaks to Me About My Witness

by
Charles "Chic" Shaver

Beacon Hill Press of Kansas City
Kansas City, Missouri

ISBN: 083-411-4046

Printed in the
United States of America

Cover Design: Royce Ratcliff

10   9   8   7   6   5   4   3   2   1

Dedication

To my children

    Rachel

    Paul

    Miriam

Who have brought me great joys,
For whom I have great love,
For whom I pray big prayers.

Contents

Preface

Could we walk together in a discovery of "witness"? I have tried to deal with biblical issues about witness in a way that would speak to people like you and me. I've hoped and prayed the "speak" would be strong enough to improve our witness—to make a difference. You will discover this pattern over and over again: from Bible to everyday life.

I have written as if we were friends. I have talked freely about "you" and "I" and "we." Where an issue in effective witness has become a concern for me, I have written about it—even, in a few cases, where the biblical teachings were more indirect than direct. Yet there are still other issues that need attention, but they will need to be saved for another day.

But today, a challenge! Let the *Bible speak* to *me* about my *witness.*

1

Soul-Winning Eyes

Who Is a Witness?

The spring day was hot and muggy. My wife and I were on a short-term teaching and preaching assignment in Greater Manila, Philippines. Our home base was an upstairs apartment on the seminary campus.

A young woman appeared at our door asking for work. Her name was Janet,[1] and she wondered if we needed a maid. At the missionaries' urging we hired her—the going rate in that area is 10 pesos, or 36 cents an hour. Janet had a husband and three children. Her home was without water, electricity, or refrigeration, with dirt for a floor.

I thought a lot about Janet. She was a gracious and helpful presence in our home away from home. I knew she previously worked for other missionaries. Their lives and words no doubt prepared her for Jesus.

One day as I was crossing the campus, the Holy Spirit said, "You have given her a job. Will you tell her about Jesus too?" I invited her to join Nancy and me for lunch the next day. During our time together we learned that through the loving witness of previous missionaries, Janet made a commitment to Christ but had fallen away. After only a few minutes of conversation, Janet began to cry. Her relationship with

Jesus was not what it should be. There at the lunch table she prayed, renewing her commitment to God. The next Sunday, Janet went to church and knelt at the altar as public testimony of her changed life.

Over the next weeks we watched Janet grow spiritually. When we left Manila, she said through tears, "I'm sorry you're going, but I'm happy in the Lord." Janet renewed her commitment to Christ because we were *witnesses*.

Soul-winning eyes see things other eyes don't see. Soul-winning eyes understand Jesus. He said, "Do you not say, 'Four months more and then the harvest'? I tell you, open your eyes and look at the fields! They are ripe for harvest" (John 4:35). Soul-winning eyes see people needing the Savior and those ready to receive Him.

What is a witness? I am a Christian witness when I tell another person what Jesus means to me and what He has done for me. After the demon-possessed man had been delivered by Jesus, he wanted to travel with the Lord to His next ministry assignment. Instead, Jesus said, "Go home to your family and tell them how much the Lord has done for you" (Mark 5:19).

Notice the elements of good witness included in Jesus' instruction. First, we are to go to our *family*—the people we best understand and with whom we have the most rapport. Second, we are to *tell*. Though people will notice our changed life, it is still necessary to tell who made the change—Jesus! Third, we are to stress *how much* the Lord has done for us. Our testimony should highlight the positive benefits Christ has brought to our life. Fourth, we are to emphasize the *Lord.* The focus is not what we have done for God but what He has done for us.

Witnessing is personal. You are telling your story. You are sharing your experience. Sometimes a witness is indirect. You are telling what Christ has done for another. But the most easily understood and effective witness is *your* story. When Peter stressed his personal experience, his testimony was so powerful that the Jewish religious authorities of the day commanded him to stop speaking about Jesus. Peter replied, "We cannot help speaking about what we have seen and heard" (Acts 4:20).

Witnessing is telling another what Jesus means to me and has done for me. There is another term we need to understand, the term *soul winning*. Soul winning is attempting to bring people to a personal acceptance of Christ as Savior and Lord. Soul winning presents the facts of the gospel and calls for a decision. It is more thorough than witnessing and involves some explanation of biblical truths needed for one's salvation. It involves an element of persuasion. Witnessing may consist of a one-sentence testimony: "John, I can only say that in the place of an empty life, Christ has given me purpose and meaning." Almost all soul winning involves witness, but a witness does not always result in immediate soul winning. The Christian's hope is that the end result of a witness is a soul is won to Christ.

In the New Testament there are three words used for spreading the Christian message by word. One is to "proclaim," another is to "tell good news" (connected to our word "evangelize"), and the third is to "bear witness."[2] The word "witness" was used primarily as a legal term. A witness was one who personally experienced and accurately reported facts or events. Or a witness vouched for the truth of a thing. Sometimes people bear witness, sometimes God or the Spirit bears witness.[3]

The Old Testament calls God's people to witness for Him against speechless idols. Isa. 43:12 states, "'I have revealed and saved and proclaimed—I, and not some foreign god among you. You are my witnesses,' declares the Lord, 'that I am God.'" The resurrected Christ urged His disciples to witness in Luke 24:46-49:

> This is what is written: The Christ will suffer and rise from the dead on the third day, and repentance and forgiveness of sins will be preached in his name to all nations, beginning at Jerusalem. You are witnesses of these things. I am going to send you what my Father has promised; but stay in the city until you have been clothed with power from on high.

The early New Testament use of the word "witness" was limited to those who knew Jesus in His earthly ministry and resurrection. Michael Green, author of *Evangelism in the Early Church*, says that limitation was eventually removed. A sense of personal encounter with the risen Jesus became the basis for genuine witness.[4] That means people like you and me— who have met the living Christ—can be His witnesses.

John's Gospel is a book filled with witness. Jesus gives witness to His own person. The Father, the miracles, the Scriptures, all bear witness to Jesus. In addition, there is an internal witness of the Spirit to those who accept the testimony.[5] Indeed John's whole purpose is to witness for Christ. His goal is bringing people to experience the life Christ gives. John exclaimed, "But these are written that you may believe that Jesus is the Christ, the Son of God, and that by believing you may have life in his name" (John 20:31).

Witness as a term from the courtroom must not mislead us. The Christian witness needs a different spirit from the argument of the court. Let's put it this way:

> The witness does not see himself or herself as a winner of arguments, but as a winner of people to Christ. The witness is going to hungry and needy people with joyous life-changing news. The prospect is not an enemy to be fought, but a person to be loved and won. It's not so much like arguing a case in a

courtroom, but wooing and winning the girl, finally persuaded to be my wife.[6]

God's Concern for the Lost

When I was five years old, my parents sent me to Sunday School with a six-year-old neighbor girl. One set of parents took us to Sunday School, and the other set picked us up. One Sunday there was a mix-up. No one picked us up. The six-year-old, sensing her maturity, was sure she could lead me home. After all, it was only a mile-and-a-half walk in a small city of 32,000. We started south, but our homes were actually east. About an hour later, my frantic mother and two frightened kids were reunited outside the police station. To this day, the fear of being lost still haunts me. There are people in our world who are lost—apart from God—and uneasy because of it.

When Jesus prayed for His disciples in John 17:11, He addressed God as "Holy Father." God is holy. People without grace are sinful. There is a gap between a holy God and sinful people. God is also Father. He loves us, and He is patiently trying to reach us in our lostness.

Matthew's Gospel was written especially to Jews. For this reason, he shows how Christians are Abraham's seed. The ancient promise of Genesis 15 is honored: "Count the stars . . . So shall your offspring be" (v. 5). As the spiritual descendants of Abraham today, we are to "go and make disciples of all nations" (Matt. 28:19). So strongly does the God of the universe and the ages feel this that through Matthew, He teaches us to see (9:36), to care (v. 36), to pray (v. 38), to receive (10:19-20), and to go (vv. 5-6).[7]

Concern for our sin (Rom. 3:23) and spiritual death (6:23) caused God to make a way for us to come to Him. Christ tells us, "For God so loved the world that he gave his one and only

Son, that whoever believes in him shall not perish but have eternal life" (John 3:16). Conversely, "Whoever rejects the Son will not see life, [but] God's wrath remains on him" (v. 36).

Some have asked if people can be saved without Christ. Robert Coleman answers that such knowledge has not been disclosed to us. God may do what He wants, within His nature, but we can only act on the word of Scripture that He has revealed to the world.[8] To teach people to expect another way of salvation is dangerous, says Robertson McQuilkin. A Christian witness may be compared to a security guard whose job is to protect the 10th-floor residents of a nursing home. He has a floor plan with the fire exits all marked. What if fire breaks out? Can you imagine the guard discussing with the residents the possibility of other escape routes besides those on the map?[9]

Some today are teaching that because God loves, He forgives everyone, under all circumstances. Henry Cook says these teachers have "emptied his love of all its desperate seriousness, and have made the cross unintelligible. If God is so kind as to forgive under any circumstances why did Jesus have to die?"[10]

If God sent His Son to die for us, then we who follow Christ must be concerned for the lost. Michael Green says,

> Now if you believe that outside of Christ there is no hope, it is impossible to possess an atom of human love . . . without being gripped by a great desire to bring men to this one way of salvation. We are not surprised, therefore, to find that concern for the state of the unevangelized was one of the great driving forces behind Christian preaching . . . in the early church.[11]

Christ summarized His ministry this way: "The Son of Man came to seek and to save what was lost" (Luke 19:10). To His followers Christ says, "As the Father has sent me, I am sending you" (John 20:21).

Jesus' concern for lost mankind was so great that He told the parables of the lost sheep, the lost coin, and the lost son in Luke 15. Here we learn no one is so worthless but that the Lord is deeply concerned for him or her (v. 4). No effort is to be spared to recover the lost (v. 4). Nothing brings as much joy to Christ and to all of heaven as when one sinner repents (vv. 7, 10). Notice the great *searching love* displayed in Jesus and the Father in these parables. His love actively seeks us even in our separation from Him.

Seth and his three sons, Mark, Milton, and Matt, owned and operated a large cattle ranch in the southwestern United States. Because the ranch included mountainous areas at an elevation of more than 7,000 feet, winter storms could develop suddenly and without much warning. Seth's family had a winter emergency plan just in case this happened.

One day a storm moved in faster than the weatherman predicted. Seth immediately implemented his plan. He designated their home as headquarters. The four then left in different directions to secure the ranch. The corrals were to be opened for the cattle to come in. Water was to be made available. They were all to meet promptly back at headquarters in two hours. The absence of one man after two hours was the signal he was in trouble.

They left early in the morning. With a hard wind blowing, both snow and the temperature were falling fast. It was a typical southwestern blizzard. After two hours, three men returned to the ranch house. Mark did not arrive. Seth and his two sons waited nervously around the fireplace to get warm. After 15 minutes passed, Seth put on his coat again. "Wait here," he told his boys. "You're finished. I'm going out to look for Mark!"

His middle son stopped him at the door: "Dad, until everybody's home, nobody's finished!" The three went to search together. They followed the designated route. Soon they saw Mark, his truck blown off the road and stuck in the snow. In a short time, Dad and all three boys were at the ranch home— safe, around the fire's warmth.

Can you see that God is like this? Whether it is seeking the lost sheep, the lost coin, or the father running out to meet the lost son, the truth is the same. *"Till everybody's home, nobody's finished!"* The Father isn't finished. The Son isn't finished. The Spirit isn't finished. I'm not finished. You're not finished. As long as there is a lost friend or loved one or lost person anywhere, *"Till everybody's home, nobody's finished!"*[12]

Every Christian's Business

When my wife, Nancy, was a little girl, her grandmother asked her to go out to the garden and dig 3 potatoes for supper. The neighbor boy, Edward Zimmerman, joined her in the task. Digging potatoes was fun. It was so much fun that instead of digging 3, they harvested 30! Somehow Grandmother did not believe reinserting 27 potatoes in the ground would produce further growth. Nancy received a spanking she still remembers—for disobeying the harvest instructions.

Jesus Christ gave His disciples harvest instructions. His concern was not that there would be too early a harvest, but that there were too few workers to finish the job. The words He spoke then issue a challenge for us today. "Ask the Lord of the harvest, therefore, to send out workers into his harvest field" (Matt. 9:38). Note that Jesus' plea is not for preachers, but workers. Obviously both laity and clergy are needed.

The world is Christ's harvest field. He has a claim on it. He is already at work within it. He has a right to direct the harvest operation. Though God has sufficient power to directly convert people to himself, He has chosen us as the means of bringing people into right relationship with Him. Philip (a layman) was led by the Spirit to ask the Ethiopian, "Do you understand what you are reading?" The Ethiopian responded, "How can I . . . unless someone explains it to me?" (Acts 8:30-31). And this "except some man should guide me," as King James puts it, is the pattern of New Testament evangelism. God uses people to bring other people into right relationship with himself.[13]

One day Jesus went for a walk by the lake. There He saw two fishermen named Peter and Andrew casting a net into the water. "'Come, follow me,' Jesus said, 'and I will make you fishers of men'" (Matt. 4:19). A short time later Jesus called James and John, also fishermen, to follow Him. They obeyed. Only the call of Matthew is described later in his Gospel (9:9). Thus "these four are intended to be taken as typical of the discipleship group."[14] They were not professional clergy, nor of great scholarship, influence, wealth, or social background. They were working-class people with no great background and no great future.[15] That means people like you and me can qualify.

Jesus did not expect them to become fishers of men on their own. He said *He would make* them fishers of men—if they followed Him. I am encouraged that the closer I follow Him, the more He will mold and shape me to be a fisher of men. The disciples used such skills as patience, perseverance, courage, and sensitivity. They matched the bait to the fish and kept themselves out of sight. Those same qualities were a part of their witnessing skills, and they should be a part of ours.

It is distressing to note that a Campus Crusade for Christ survey reveals that 98 percent of professing Christians do not regularly share their faith. The Alban Institute on Church

Growth discovered that in mainline Protestantism, a person is invited to church by someone once every 28 years.[16]

When Jesus called Matthew to follow Him, the tax collector threw a big dinner party for the Lord (Matt. 9:9-13). He invited his tax collector friends and other sinners. He wanted them to meet Jesus. To want our friends to meet Christ should be natural, and for everybody, not just evangelism specialists or clergy.

Preaching is the ministry of a few who are called and so gifted. Witnessing, however, is a method available *to all Christians*. The rapid spread of Christianity in the Early Church was due in large part to the witness of lay Christians.[17] Origen, the Early Church historian, states, "Christians do all in their power to spread the faith over the world."[18] Evangelist Leighton Ford says, "A church which bottlenecks its outreach by depending on its specialists—its pastors and evangelists—to do its witnessing, is living in violation of both the intention of its Head and the consistent pattern of early Christians."[19]

Acts 8:4 tells of the spread of early Christianity: "Those who had been scattered preached the word wherever they went." However, verse 1 more clearly defines who was doing all this preaching: "On that day a great persecution broke out against the church at Jerusalem, and all except the apostles were scattered throughout Judea and Samaria." In other words, the apostles stayed in Jerusalem. It was the laity who were scattered and spread the Word.

While it is true some people have the gift of evangelism, every Christian is called to witness (Luke 24:48 and Acts 1:8). And while we need the ministries of nurture to those already Christian, there is the need for starting new life. We dare not be just "keepers of the aquarium" when Jesus calls us *all* to be "fishers of men."

How I See People

If you had to deal with a complaining boss or a crabby teacher this week, what do you think he or she needs? It may be natural to respond, "He or she needs someone to tell him or her off!" Did you ever think that he or she needs Jesus?

The disciples went to a Samaritan town to buy food (John 4:8). On their return they were amazed to find Jesus witnessing to a Samaritan woman (v. 27). It was more of a shock when many of the Samaritans responded to Christ because of the woman's testimony (v. 39). The disciples had been shopping from some of these same people and apparently had only thought of the quality and price of their groceries. Evidently they left no witness.

During this event, Jesus talked to the disciples about soul-winning eyes. We read about this in John 4:34-38.

> "My food," said Jesus, "is to do the will of him who sent me and to finish his work. Do you not say, 'Four months more and then the harvest'? I tell you, open your eyes and look at the fields! They are ripe for harvest. Even now the reaper draws his wages, even now he harvests the crop for eternal life, so that the sower and the reaper may be glad together. Thus the saying 'One sows and another reaps' is true. I sent you to reap what you have not worked for. Others have done the hard work, and you have reaped the benefits of their labor."

These verses teach:

1. Christ's greatest satisfaction was to win people to himself and the Kingdom (v. 34).
2. In the field of people around you, there are some ready to accept Christ now (v. 35).
3. You do not have to do all the work in order to reap. Someone else may sow the seed. This prepares the person to receive Christ (vv. 36-37).

4. Both sowers and reapers are valuable to God (vv. 36-37).
5. If you do reap, you must not take credit. Someone else has done the hard work of preparation (v. 38).

As Beverly prepared for Sunday morning church service, she prayed she would meet someone she could influence for Jesus. That same morning Sharon got in her car and began driving. She was hurting and needed help. She thought church might be the answer. That morning Beverly and Sharon arrived at the same church. They struck up a conversation and started a friendship. In only a short time Beverly witnessed to Sharon and had the privilege of seeing her accept Christ. Sharon was ripe for harvest, and Beverly was looking for the harvest. She was seeing people with soul-winning eyes.

People may appear tired, lonely, or even jubilant as we meet them. But there's more—each individual has a spiritual condition as well. He or she is:

—in one of two realms: darkness or light
—under one of two powers: Satan or God
—traveling one of two ways: broad way or narrow way
—in one of two relationships: against Christ or for Christ
—in one of two groupings: tares or wheat
—going to one of two destinies: hell or heaven
—either: dead or alive
—either: lost or found

Many who don't know Christ are hungry to find Him.

Sadly, there are those who profess love for Jesus, yet winning another person to Christ never crosses their minds. Oh, that God will give them soul-winning eyes. May we all begin to see others as people for whom Jesus died.

When you see people with soul-winning eyes, your love

for them is deep enough that you want to affect their eternal destiny. Your eyes of concern will realize they are trapped in sin. They may invite you to participate in actions that are not right. It is important to determine what habits you will practice as a Christian. It is also important to keep them consistently. Our world laughs at inconsistency. Even though we may have settled the issues of personal convictions, we must not *condemn* the person for whom we are concerned.

Imagine you have only recently met Jim through work. You are working a construction job together and are carpooling. On the way home from work your first day together, Jim is driving. He says, "Boy, it's been hot today. Let's stop for a cold beer." Let's assume that as a Christian you have a conviction against the use of alcoholic beverages. How will you answer him? You might say, "No thanks, Jim. I don't drink. I'm a Christian." But that answer may sound like you are condemning him. Consider the following answer: "No thanks, Jim. I don't drink. But you know, my wife and I would like very much to get to know you and your wife better. Would there be an evening next week where we could have you over for dinner?"

The guideline here is clear: If an unsaved person suggests a wrong activity to you, with your refusal suggest an alternative activity. From this, the person will know you are not rejecting him or her. In Jesus' conversation with the Samaritan woman (John 4:4-26), He carefully built a friendship with her before dealing with her sin.

Soul-winning eyes not only will cause us to look at individuals differently but also will affect our decisions about organizations and strategy. In a recent visit to Korea, my wife and I met a Korean pastor. Pastor Lee at the An-Jung church told us that in his village of 10,000 people there were 2 Nazarene churches. Recently he had received 25 new members, bringing his present church membership to 785. This is the daughter church of the In-Kwang church. While it is smaller than the An-Jung church, the In-Kwang church has started 16 daughter churches. The In-Kwang church has soul-winning eyes, believing that all across that region churches must be planted. No wonder there has been such rapid church growth in this region of Korea. They have soul-winning eyes.

Soul-winning eyes, or seeing people as people for whom Christ died, results in a passion for souls. District Superintendent Wil Spaite notes that though the Church of the Nazarene was one of the two fastest-growing denominations in the 1930s, there was little organized training. In recent years we have had a great increase in seminars and training.

Our recent gains, however, have only been 1 to 3 percent a year in the United States. Dr. Spaite is glad for the improved training of today, but he wonders what Nazarenes of the '30s had that was so special. He believes,

> It was because most of the Nazarenes had a *caring love to see the lost won to Christ.* The eternal destiny of family, friends, and neighbors was so much on their hearts that *they loved them to Christ.* [20]

This is what I mean by a passion for souls, and it must be cultivated anew. The passion for souls was with Abraham as he pleaded with God for Lot and Sodom. It was with Jesus as He wept over Jerusalem. It was with Paul who said, "Brothers, my heart's desire and prayer to God for the Israelites is that they may be saved" (Rom. 10:1). Is it a part of your life?

As I was going through the checkout counter at my favorite drugstore, I was distressed by a man in front of me purchasing a pornographic magazine. I decided to speak to the druggist about it. I'd built a little friendship with him and felt I could say something. I said, "Everett, I like your store. I have the feeling you want to help me. You provide medicine and products that promote health and heal my body. That's why it concerns me that you would sell something that poisons the mind."

I had his interest. He asked me what I meant. I told him about the magazine. He told me to whom I should write in the company, and I did. The magazine was removed from the shelves.

But dealing with the social evil of pornography is not enough. I am concerned for Everett's spiritual welfare as well. At a later time in the store I visited with Everett again. I complimented him on his helpfulness. I asked if he and his wife had a church home they attended regularly. He said they didn't, and I invited them to attend my church. They responded to my invitation. Not long after, I visited the pharmacy again. I heard that Everett's son, Eugene, was getting out of the military. I asked Eugene if he would be willing to talk to my church youth group about Vietnam. He did.

Ten years passed, and I was teaching at the seminary in Kansas City. As my class was leaving the room, a tall, good-looking guy walked in. He stuck out his hand. "Remember me?" he asked.

"I'm Eugene. The first time I ever attended the Nazarene church was at your invitation. Since then I've been saved, joined the church, and now I'm in seminary studying for the ministry."

I'm glad I went to the drugstore that day with soul-winning eyes. Be sure you are seeing with soul-winning eyes. Someone you know needs Jesus now.[21] Jesus said, "I tell you, open your eyes and look at the fields! They are ripe for harvest." Another has said, "We shall have all eternity to worship—but only this lifetime to witness."[22]

Your Response

Your concern must become action. List five people you know who need Jesus now. Be sure at least three of them are near enough to you that they might come to your local church. Begin praying that God will draw them to himself. Pray He will help you witness to them.

1. _____

2. _____

3. _____

4. _____

5. _____

2

Witness out of the Overflow

My friend Peter Gunas witnessed to me in my room at Dartmouth College. He told me the greatest before and after story I had ever heard, and Christ was the Agent of change. On November 20, 1955, at 9 P.M. in the Claremont, N.H., Church of the Nazarene under the ministry of Ralph Ferrioli, I met Jesus Christ. What a change! My perception of life changed from night to day, from sadness to gladness, all in a moment.

Within hours I thought, I've got to tell my loved ones about this. *Since Christ has done so much for me, I have to tell them about Him.* They too could be forgiven and know God personally. I began to pray that each of my blood relatives would come to know the Lord. I went home and told my mom. That next summer, she came to radiantly know the Savior and was saved from sin and delivered from suicidal tendencies.

Why Witness?

Our motive for witnessing should be loving gratitude. In *Evangelism in the Early Church,* Michael Green points out that the main motive for evangelism among early Christians was the sense of gratitude for what Christ had done for them. He says, "Magnetized by this love, their lives could not but show it, their lips could not help telling it; 'we cannot but speak of the things which we have seen and heard.'"[1]

John wrote, "Dear friends, since God so loved us, we also ought to love one another" (1 John 4:11). That meant Christians must live lives of loving works.

John went on to write, "And we have seen and *testify* that the Father has sent his Son to be the Savior of the world" (v. 14, italics mine). That meant that Christians must give verbal witness or testimony to Christ. Both the works and the words flow from God's prior love. The main motive for witness among early Christians was, according to Green, "because of the overwhelming experience of the love of God which they had received through Jesus Christ."[2]

Loving gratitude as the driving force for witnessing is important to grasp. It is frequently assumed that the direct command of Christ in the Great Commission of Matt. 28:18-20 was the motivation behind early witnessing and evangelism. In fact, the Great Commission was quoted very little in the second century. I believe the Great Commission is important. Its importance is not because it is a harsh command to be kept, however, but because that command expresses the heart mission of those touched by Christ.[3] Early Christians obeyed the Great Commission from a natural overflowing love created within by Christ, not a forced obedience.

Responsibility toward God (John 8:29; 2 Cor. 5:9-11), concern for the lost (Matt. 7:13-14), and concern over the coming of Christ (1 Thess. 1:5-10) were motives for evangelism. To witness is to be like God. Wayne Ward says, "Evangelism grows out of the very nature of God himself who in his great love reaches down in Jesus Christ to reconcile sinful men unto himself."[4]

Love for God more than love for the lost must motivate

our witness. If our focus is people, then evangelism loses its central power, which is the presence of God. Remember Jesus asked Peter, "Do you love *me?*" (John 21:17, italics mine). Then He said, "Feed my sheep." He did not ask, "Do you love the *sheep?*" The focus was on Christ. Rom. 5:5 gives the secret: "God has poured out his love into our hearts by the Holy Spirit, whom he has given us." Someone has defined witness as "one beggar telling another beggar where to find bread." In the light of what Jesus has done for you and me, shouldn't we be telling others how to find Him? If we love enough, we will find a way!

A Daily Relationship

"Unless we believe that what's happened to us in our relationship with Christ ought to happen to everyone, then probably too little has happened to us," proclaims Lloyd Ogilvie. As loving gratitude is the major motive for witness, so our relationship with Christ is the source of witness. A present, daily relationship with Christ is essential to this process.

Jesus taught that fishing for men was a result of *ongoing following* with Him (Matt. 4:19). The Vine and branches teaching of John 15 speaks of reproduction only as there is moment-by-moment sustenance from the Source. Jesus said, "I am the vine; you are the branches. If a man remains in me and I in him, he will bear much fruit" (v. 5). Our spiritual life—and our ultimate salvation—are dependent on a continuing relationship with Christ. In verse 6, Jesus continues, "If anyone does not remain in me, he is like a branch that is thrown away and withers; such branches are picked up, thrown into the fire and burned." This theme is reiterated in other Gospels. Michael Green, in *Matthew for Today*, commenting on Matt. 13:47-50, says: "There is no trace in Matthew of any doctrine that we can have instant salvation apart from constant perseverance. We must be righteous and live with the Righteous one."[5]

I came to Christ while I was a student at an Ivy League college. Much about my college was not a friend to grace. My faith was often challenged. I dared not leave my room any morning to face either problems or people until I first faced God. The Psalmist taught me, "In the morning, O Lord, you hear my voice" (5:3). The habit of a regular daily time with my Heavenly Father has become a major factor in maintaining a daily relationship for me.

Rev. Ray Matson says it is impossible to move people's hearts on six minutes a day in prayer.[6] His words encourage us to move increasingly into a ministry of intercession. Could we be so bold as to pray for the spiritual awakening defined by David Bryant:

> When the Father wakes us up to see Christ's fullness in new ways, so that together we trust Him, love Him, and obey Him in new ways, so that we move with Him in new ways for the fulfillment of His global cause?[7]

A person in daily relationship with Christ reads the Scripture with the expectation of being changed. Richard Foster has reminded us, "The central purpose of the work of Scripture is the transforming of life, not to amass information."[8] Let us hold ourselves accountable to the demands of the grace-filled Word.

Is it possible to live in daily spiritual renewal? Yes, as we learn to practice the presence of God. When I face temptations, I say, "Lord Jesus, You live in me, and You are willing to release Your power through me." When I need to have my faith strengthened, I remember the words of Hudson Taylor, "Not by striving after faith, but by resting on the Faithful One." When I face a new day, I recall George Mueller's statement: "I consider it my greatest need before God and man to get my soul happy before the Lord each day before I see anybody." If I see sin in my life, I remember God never reveals sin except to remove it by Christ's cleansing blood (1 John 1:7). When I look within, I practice Robert Murray McCheyne's advice: "For every look you take at yourself, take 10 at Jesus Christ." Paul Little said, "Inner spiritual reality developed by a secret life with God is essential for an effective witness to a pagan world."[9] 2 Pet. 1:3 proclaims, "His divine power has given us everything we need for life and godliness through our knowledge of him."

Mike Mason and his wife had just had their first child, but Mike wasn't very happy. The company for which he had worked 20 years had laid him off along with many other senior employees. Although he had searched regularly for a new job, he would receive only two more unemployment checks. I suggested he come to the early morning men's prayer meeting held Fridays at our church and ask the men to pray. At 7:15 A.M. we prayed. At 8:30 A.M. he phoned a company where he had put in his job application only to be told there was no opening. At 1:40 P.M., a representative from the same company called back: "Mike, you have the job!" He was one of 400 applicants. Mike was excited. He began to praise the Lord. He phoned his mom to tell her God answers prayer. He phoned his friends and praised the Lord. It was a natural witness flowing out of God's answer to his prayer.

It wouldn't be hard to witness with an answer like that, would it? Consider Ann. She is a committed wife and mother. She prays daily. But recently her husband left her. Yet, Ann stood in a Sunday School class and witnessed to God's keeping presence and power in her life. No matter what our circumstances, witness and daily relationship with Christ go together!

Often Christian workers can be trapped into thinking that their Christian service can substitute for their devotion. I am helped by the words of Lois Lebar: "Never let service for Jesus take the place of fellowship with Jesus."

The Spirit and Witness

You will be discouraged in your attempts to be a witness unless you realize the Holy Spirit is the Great Evangelist of the Trinity. He is the Master Evangelist in the world. While you speak to a person's ears what Jesus means to you, the Holy Spirit speaks to the person's heart. Jesus said, "No one can come to me unless the Father who sent me draws him" (John 6:44). The *Father is drawing.* Jesus promised the Holy Spirit would "convict the world of guilt in regard to sin and righteousness and judgment" (16:8). The *Spirit is convicting.* Jesus said, "But when he, the Spirit of truth, comes, he will guide you into all truth. . . . He will bring glory to me" (vv. 13-14). The *Spirit is bringing glory to Jesus.* Jesus taught that "when the Counselor comes, . . . he will testify about me" (15:26). The *Spirit is testifying about Jesus.* Verse 27 continues, "And you also must testify." F. F. Bruce says, "John and his associates bear witness to the truth of what they have seen and heard" (1 John 1:2-3; 4:14), "but behind their witness lies the witness of the Spirit" (3:24; 4:13).[10]

The one-two punch of the person's witness and the Spirit's witness is demonstrated in Acts 5:32, "We are witnesses of these things, and so is the Holy Spirit, whom God has given to those who obey him." There are at least 41 references to the Holy Spirit's working in the Book of Acts. There are 29 other references specifically to divine leadership, frequently references to the leadership of the Spirit. Commonly, an Acts reference combines the Spirit's work with help in speaking God's message. As 4:31 reads, "After they prayed, . . . they were all filled with the Holy Spirit and spoke the word of God boldly." Are you starting to believe that God's Spirit will help you witness?

Green says, "God's gift of His Spirit was intended not to make them comfortable but to make them witnesses."[11] Again: "Every initiative in evangelism recorded in Acts is the initiative of the Spirit of God."[12]

I was scared. A new Christian, I was increasingly uncomfortable with my membership in a national Greek letter fraternity at my college. I had recently read in the Word, "Do not be yoked together with unbelievers" (2 Cor. 6:14). The fraternity was built on principles of secrecy and snobbishness. Whether I wanted it or not, my social tax helped buy their beer. I went to the vice president and told him I felt I must leave the fraternity because of my Christian convictions. He was understanding, but he said I did not have the right to decide, and neither did the local fraternity executives. I had to go before the all-college interfraternity council.

I feared they would never understand. This council was made up of 12 fraternity men, and 6 were fraternity presidents. I knew they'd brand me some kind of a nut if I said I wanted to leave my fraternity for religious reasons. But there was no other way. The date for my meeting was set. I was in my room before the appointment, nervous, wondering what to say, and trying to get the Lord's help. I was reading in Luke, and 21:14-15 lit up for me: "But make up your mind not to worry beforehand how you will defend yourselves. For I will give you words and wisdom that none of your adversaries will be able to resist or contradict."

I believed those words meant that God, by His Spirit, would especially help me speak to the council.

As I sat in the waiting room outside the council chambers, I fretted anxiously. It was already 25 minutes past my appointment time. I leaned over to the man sitting next to me. Timidly I asked, "Are you wanting to get out of your fraternity?" "Yes," he responded, "I've gotten married, and I'd like to get out of the fraternity so that I could live with my wife." Oh, boy! I thought, I hope he doesn't ask my reason.

At that moment, it seemed the Lord moved into the room at ceiling level. He maneuvered till He was right over me. Suddenly He dumped the whole bucket of peace into my heart. Just then the big oak door opened. A voice: "Mr. Shaver, we're ready for you." I was ready for them too. A member of the council asked why I wanted to leave the fraternity. It seemed the only thing I could do was give my witness. I told them that Jesus had become my Savior, had changed me, and had given me a sensitivity to issues that had never bothered me before. Most of them were upset by what I said. Eventually they ended the meeting by saying, "We'll write you a letter and let you know if we are going to dismiss you from your fraternity." In three days I had a letter giving permission to leave my fraternity. The next year the same fraternity invited me back to speak to a house meeting about what it meant to be a Christian! Indeed, I was discovering that the Spirit intended not to make me comfortable but to make me a witness.

The resurrected Christ told His disciples that repentance and forgiveness of sins would be preached in His name to all nations. He went on to explain their role in the process: "You are witnesses of these things. I am going to send you what my Father has promised; but stay in the city until you have been clothed with power from on high" (Luke 24:48-49).

Our focus is witness and the power to do it. That concern was answered in one of the most important witnessing verses of the Bible, Acts 1:8: "But you will receive power when the

Holy Spirit comes on you; and you will be my witnesses in Jerusalem, and in all Judea and Samaria, and to the ends of the earth."

Jesus was concerned for His disciples. He urged them to seek the Spirit's fullness and power. On occasion He had rebuked them for their pettiness, selfishness, and concern for position (Matt. 20:20-28). As He faced the Cross, He carried a great burden for the Twelve.

In John 17:17, Jesus prayed for His disciples, "Sanctify them by the truth; your word is truth." In verse 20, He continued, "My prayer is not for them alone. I pray also for those who will believe in me through their message." In this prayer Jesus interceded for His generation and ours. Our generation comes to Christ through a message carried from the first generation. The cost of delivering that message is so extreme that only the person fully yielded and fully cleansed will be faithful. Jesus' prayer for the disciples' sanctification helps remove the lingering barriers of selfishness in their lives. He risked His whole cause on these 12 men. Our generation is forced to face the same issues, because the next generation depends on our passing on the message. People simply quit when the going gets rough unless the fire on the inside is greater than the pressure on the outside.

The disciples were "filled with the Holy Spirit" on the Day of Pentecost (Acts 2:4). Peter says that God also "purified their hearts by faith" (15:9). That's another way to say they were sanctified entirely. To be filled with the Spirit is the standard of Christian experience. Once a person has been filled with the Spirit, it is important to remain in that state. Eph. 5:18 is written in the present tense: *"Be* filled with the Spirit," which means, *keep* filled with the Spirit. Some Christians have been justified freely but have not yet been sanctified entirely. They have been born of the Spirit but not filled with the Spirit. And there are those who were once filled with the Spirit who today are not. Are you Spirit-filled just now?[13]

A Man Who Was Filled with the Spirit

Philip was a layman chosen to serve on the first local church board. The board was created because there was need for food distribution among Grecian Jewish widows. The primary qualification for election to the board was to be full of the Spirit and wisdom. Apparently not all early Christians were Spirit-filled, or there would have been no need to specify this condition for election (Acts 6:1-5). When Stephen was stoned to death and the Church scattered, Philip went to Samaria and proclaimed Christ (8:1-8). He continued to live the Spirit-filled life, and God used him powerfully. Consider the account in verses 26-39:

[26]Now an angel of the Lord said to Philip, "Go south to the road—the desert road—that goes down from Jerusalem to Gaza." [27]So he started out, and on his way he met an Ethiopian eunuch, an important official in charge of all the treasury of Candace, queen of the Ethiopians. This man had gone to Jerusalem to worship, [28]and on his way home was sitting in his chariot reading the book of Isaiah the prophet. [29]The Spirit told Philip, "Go to that chariot and stay near it."

[30]Then Philip ran up to the chariot and heard the man reading Isaiah the prophet. "Do you understand what you are reading?" Philip asked.

[31]"How can I," he said, "unless someone explains it to me?" So he invited Philip to come up and sit with him.

[32]The eunuch was reading this passage of Scripture:

"He was led like a sheep to the slaughter,
    and as a lamb before the shearer is silent,
        so he did not open his mouth.
[33]In his humiliation he was deprived of justice.

Who can speak of his descendants?
For his life was taken from the earth."

³⁴The eunuch asked Philip, "Tell me, please, who is the prophet talking about, himself or someone else?" ³⁵Then Philip began with that very passage of Scripture and told him the good news about Jesus.

³⁶As they traveled along the road, they came to some water and the eunuch said, "Look, here is water. Why shouldn't I be baptized?"

³⁸And he gave orders to stop the chariot. Then both Philip and the eunuch went down into the water and Philip baptized him. ³⁹When they came up out of the water, the Spirit of the Lord suddenly took Philip away, and the eunuch did not see him again, but went on his way rejoicing.

The reasons I am convinced that Philip continued living a Spirit-filled life are:

1. Philip had to be spiritually sensitive to be preaching God's Word, seeing great numbers come to Christ (8:4-8, 14-19), and yet sense the Spirit's leadership to go to the desert (v. 26).
2. The Spirit clearly led Philip to go to the Ethiopian (v. 29).
3. Philip was immediately obedient (v. 30).
4. Philip was sensitive in dealing with the Ethiopian (vv. 30-35).
5. The Ethiopian's heart was open to the gospel message, which validated the internal leadership experienced by Philip.
6. Philip delighted to tell him the good news about Jesus.
7. The Ethiopian was converted and baptized and took the message back to Ethiopia.

Isn't that the model we want to follow? Filled with the Spirit, led by the Spirit, walking in the Spirit—and witnessing to the good news of Jesus.

Michael Green exclaims, "Until our lives have been filled with the Spirit of God, we shall not be likely to engage enthusiastically in evangelism and mission . . . The power of the Lord and the mission of the Lord belong together" (Acts 1:8).[14] Does it happen today—the fullness of the Spirit empowering people to witness? I saw it just a few weeks ago in the life of a Filipino brother. Robin Gabrido attended a discipleship group titled *Living in the Power of the Spirit.*[15] The group discussions and his personal study about the Holy Spirit caused him to recognize a lack in his Christian life. He also attended a week of revival services at Gethsemane Church, Taytay, Philippines.

One Wednesday night during revival, Robin went forward to pray. He asked God to sanctify him entirely and fill him with the Holy Spirit. He received God's answer and testified with beaming face, "My heart is purified. I am so happy. I could sing. I could shout. I want to be with my Christian brothers and sisters."

Robin's concern went beyond Christian brothers and sisters. At the next discipleship group, he reported that he had been enemies with his brother for 10 years over a business disagreement. Since the Holy Spirit had filled Robin, he had been praying for his brother. One night Robin arrived home, and his brother was waiting for him. His brother apologized, and they were reconciled. Robin and his wife, Elena, witnessed to the brother. He accepted Christ. Within another week the two families got together again for a meal. In our final discipleship group, Robin gave one last report to the group: "Before, I was ashamed to talk to people about Christ. Now I have courage. I'm amazed—I've talked to three people about the Lord, and they've all been converted. I feel like I'm a winner with my Lord."

The Spirit's fullness and power for witness. How good!

For Philip—a man filled with the Spirit! For Robin—a man filled with the Spirit! For you and me!

Back to the Place of Prayer

Two amazing practices characterized the early Christians —they were people of prayer, and they were led by the Spirit. The early history of the Church, the Book of Acts, shows that church life was conducted in an atmosphere of prayer. There are at least 34 references to prayer in Acts. In conjunction with prayer it is important to recognize the openness of Christians to hear the Spirit's prompting. Most all of the 29 references to divine leadership in Acts are related to evangelistic witness or strategy. Philip is led to the Ethiopian (8:29-30), Ananias is led to Saul (9:10-17), Peter is guided to Cornelius (10:19-20). While the church is praying, fasting, and worshiping, the Holy Spirit launches the first New Testament missionary team (13:2). Indeed the privilege of believers is recorded in Rom. 8:14, "Those who are led by the Spirit of God are sons of God." So today we should discover that "research based, Spirit led strategy to reach people with the Good News and build them in the faith."[16]

When Christ saw the need of workers for His harvest field, He did not simply send them but rather asked them to go to prayer for the sending (Matt. 9:37-38). He knew that the place of prayer would cause them to face themselves before God, to be searched and purified by the Spirit. The place of prayer would keep the presence of God real in their lives. We should be careful if we pray for workers to be sent to the harvest, because the ones commanded to pray for harvest workers in chapter 9 of Matthew are the ones sent into the harvest in chapter 10! New strategies come because we repeatedly ask the Lord to send out workers into His harvest. The results will continue to magnify present-day grace.

Regular, daily return to the place of prayer is needed for our spiritual renewal. Our witness will have impact as it arises out of the Spirit's overflow in our lives. And it doesn't seem likely that we will keep filled with the Spirit unless we are people of prayer. Beyond that, prayer is part of the battle gear we use to defeat evil powers in our world (Eph. 6:10-20). Specifically, our prayer is to be "in the Spirit" (v. 18), and prayer is needed so that we "will fearlessly make known the mystery of the gospel" (v. 19).

Prayer should go both before and after our witness. Dave Wilkerson's efforts to reach street kids and see people delivered from drug addiction have seen encouraging results. Yet Wilkerson has said, "All souls won on the street are first won in prayer."[17]

Cameron Thompson illustrates the importance of the long range in prayer:

> Our prayers should be persistent. God's delays are not denials. Each day brings the answers to our prayers nearer . . . At a meeting in a small town in the United States a very old man was converted. Another old man stepped forward and with tears told how 50 years earlier 25 young people had made a pledge to pray for this man every day. Said he, "I am the only one still living to see the prayers of 50 years answered."[18]

When there seems to be no response to our witness, we still can pray. Our daughter Rachel had left her marriage, her Lord, and her church. She was living in Chicago. The pain of her decisions caused Nancy and me a great deal of heartache. I experienced an extreme feeling of sadness when I thought of Rachel.

We prayed for her salvation regularly. Months became years, and nothing seemed to happen. Then I remembered Rosalind Rinker's advice: If you don't get an answer to the big request, break it down to bite-size pieces or segments that your faith can believe for.[19] I prayed that God would drop some Christian influences into her life and that He would lead some Christian witnesses across her path. She had just gone to work at a Chicago bank with more than 1,000 employees. I was sure there must be some Christians among the 1,000.

Without thinking of my prayer, I began to send her some audiotapes of some of my sermons. Shortly she began to write us, quoting my sermons, and giving her responses. A little spark of encouragement began to glow in me. Then she reported she was getting romantically involved with a Roman Catholic man from work. I thought, "Lord, this was not exactly what I had in mind." One day she played one of my tapes for her friend, Bill. He got real serious at the end of the tape. He said, "Rachel, if I'd been there, I would have gone to the altar." Knowing Rachel's background was Church of the Nazarene, Bill checked the Chicago phone book, apparently contacted the Nazarene district office, and got directions to a local church. The next Sunday that Roman Catholic fellow took my daughter to First Church of the Nazarene, Chicago.

Over the next months and years God was working. Rachel had known the godly Howard Hamlin, medical missionary and surgeon, before his death. She read his story *This Pair of Hands*. God drew her through it. The memories of Dr. Ralph Earle, Bible scholar and translator, came across her mind. He had been especially kind to her when she was a little girl. His admonition to her as an adult, "Rachel, let God be first," was accepted. Orlan Smith, a former nightclub entertainer, found Jesus and brought his sweet saxophone to Christ. A tape of one of his saxophone solos spoke to Rachel. The Christian influences I had prayed would drop into her life were multiplying. She came to our home in Kansas City for a visit in September of 1988. One of our new converts

41

witnessed to her and told her how Jesus had changed his life. That impacted her. After my morning devotions on September 18, 1988, I said to my wife, "I could see Rachel coming to the altar when I prayed this morning."

At 9:30 in the evening, our telephone rang. It was Rachel. "Daddy, what were you doing tonight?" I said, "I was giving my testimony at St. Paul's Church." She said, "While you were giving your testimony there, I was listening to your testimony here on tape,"[20] and she began to cry. She said, "For the last half hour I've been down here beside my bed on my knees confessing my sins, and I want you to know that Jesus Christ has come into my heart, and the whole burden of sin is lifted, and I feel the best I've felt in the last five years."[21]

For the fears of facing her coworkers the next day, where her reputation as a woman of the world was well established, God gave her Phil. 4:4-7. Particularly significant were the words "Do not be anxious about anything" and "the peace of God . . . will guard your hearts and your minds in Christ Jesus."

Since that miracle night, Rachel has returned to Kansas City. She has found an outstanding job in an area pharmaceutical company, become very active in our local church, and married Kent, one of our new church members. Their hearts are touched by the cause of missions, and in a few days they will leave for their second Latin American missionary construction trip together.

I have before me a letter she wrote us five days after her conversion. Let me quote the final paragraph:

> And last but not least I have to mention you and Mom. You have not given up, you loved me and cared for me, even when I was not so lovely. Thank you for your concern and many prayers. I love you both dearly.

Today we have a brand-new daughter. Prayer was a major factor in the victory. Let us all be sure we have been back to the place of prayer. May we witness from the Spirit's overflow in our lives.

*   *   *

Your Response

You have been praying for five people who need Jesus now. You hope to witness to them. You realize your witness should flow from a rich daily relationship with Christ, empowered by the Spirit. Choose one or two trusted Christian friends (or a class that may be studying this book), and report to them once a week over the next four weeks your progress on one of the following issues:

1. What I will do to be sure I am presently a Spirit-filled, entirely sanctified Christian.

2. What I will do to establish a meaningful daily devotional time with the Lord.

3. What I will do to improve and strengthen my daily devotional time with the Lord.

3

To Whom?

One day I met a lady who lived only two blocks from my parsonage. She had a church background but no evangelical understanding. The concept of new birth was a complete mystery to her. She expressed a little openness to spiritual things. Sensing she did not know Christ, I launched into a full-blown witness of my salvation. She seemed shocked. Later she said, "You're the most sincere minister I ever met," but she never attended my church a single time.

I had failed to make any analysis of her readiness for the gospel. I saw only two groups of people—saved and unsaved. All unsaved needed to be saved, and I gave them all the same message. I have matured since this first pastorate experience, and I realize that some unsaved people are more open to the gospel than others. Prospect recognition now has an important place in my witnessing efforts. A prospect is a person who needs Jesus. He or she is a prospective receiver of the Good News. Prospect recognition is the witness's awareness of the prospect's receptivity.

Who Is Ready?

Jesus began His ministry in Galilee. This small 25 x 50-mile area was the most fertile region of Palestine. In it were 204 villages, each of which had a population of more than 15,000. Because the area was surrounded by Gentiles, was an often conquered area, and had major commercial routes passing through it, it was especially open to new ideas. Barclay calls it "the one place in all Palestine where a new teacher with a new message had any real chance of being heard."[1]

Further, Jesus started His ministry in the most comfortable setting—the synagogue (Matt. 4:23-25). Verbal address was a common part of synagogue worship, and any person recognized as suitable by the synagogue president could give it. Though His message was not always comfortable, this setting *was* comfortable for both Jesus and His hearers. This example supports the idea of laypeople giving their witness or testimony in the church. It is a comfortable setting and a good beginning place.

Not only did Jesus model a ministry that used prospect recognition, but also He taught it. In Matt. 7:6, He warned His disciples against giving sacred truths to hardened or unappreciative hearts. In 10:11-16, Jesus told them to search for a "worthy person" in the newly entered town. The groups with which the disciples should not spend much time are those who "will not welcome you or listen to your words." Jesus wanted us to be careful stewards of time, energy, and resources, saying we were to "be as shrewd as snakes and as innocent as doves." The parable of the sower (13:1-23) may be interpreted as the need to find the most productive soil. John 4:35 teaches that by observing the prospects, one should be able to tell if they are ready to accept the gospel. Jesus' approach to Nathanael in 1:47, one "in whom there is nothing false," indicates we should begin our witnessing with the best prospects, the best prepared, the most spiritually honest and hungry. Michael Green says,

Jesus goes on to warn His disciples against wasting time on the hardened . . . It is an irresponsible use of time and effort to hammer on a door that is firmly closed. The disciples should push on a door and, if it is ajar, enter in . . . Disciples of Jesus are not to be storm troopers for the Kingdom of God. They should be equipped with the most sensitive radar to see where the Spirit of God is already preparing the way, and only then move in.[2]

Even the events surrounding the witness tend to help us concentrate on the most responsive. When Paul went to Thessalonica, he followed the most comfortable pattern. Acts 17:2 says, "As his custom was, Paul went into the synagogue." In his ministry there, some Jews were persuaded, but others became jealous and opposed him. The Christians got Paul out of town as soon as possible. The next stop was Berea, and Luke notes the difference in responsiveness: "Now the Bereans were of more noble character than the Thessalonians . . . Many of the Jews believed" (vv. 10-12). It is important for us to be alert to the issue of the recognition of good prospects, because many Christians have become discouraged by spending all their witnessing efforts on a few who are obviously unresponsive. The best way to deal with a presently unresponsive person is prayer and alertness to future signs of responsiveness.

Are there any signs that indicate when a person is a good prospect and more inclined to be open to the gospel? Yes! People are more apt to be ready to accept Christ when

1. They have gone through an insecurity-producing situation.

2. They begin to discuss spiritual things.

3. They show signs of moving toward God instead of away from Him.

The Philippian jailer accepted Christ after an insecurity-producing situation, a violent earthquake (Acts 16:25-34). However, an insecurity-producing situation need not be calamity or tragedy. Happy events can have insecurity-producing overtones. It could be a new home, new neighborhood, new job, new responsibility, new marriage, new baby, new school. It may be experiences of sadness—illness, death of loved one, a compulsive alcohol or drug habit, or divorce. I saw an older man come to Christ. I tried to analyze why. Then I remembered he had just retired—a new phase of life for him. The change points of life can especially be times for people to come to Christ.

In chapter 2 I told the story of my daughter Rachel's conversion to Christ. Two years before her conversion she had attended some revival services where I had preached. One night I had an especially good talk with her. I was hoping I could prompt some spiritual discussion. Yet I had to be careful with my rebellious daughter. So I asked this question, "What do you see happening in your life in the next few years?" Her response included her support of some of the family's traditional values. After her conversion, I asked her about that conversation. She said, "I was willing to talk, but I wasn't willing to make a commitment!" Yet, the willingness to talk was a positive signal.

Church membership or religious sentiment does not necessarily mean a person is a Christian. These people may need to hear the gospel. I had been a church attender for 15 years and was a church member when someone made the gospel plain enough to me so that I could accept it.

When Paul went to Philippi, the first step he took to find prospects for the gospel was to go to a prayer meeting. There he found Lydia, already a worshiper of God but longing for more. Acts 16:14 says, "The Lord opened her heart to respond to Paul's message." She became a strong leader in the Early

Church. Paul found her when she was moving toward God.

Rev. Dale Galloway once told me that he especially noted people in the congregation who had broken a pattern of absence and suddenly showed up in church. When he called on these people, he estimated 70 percent of them accepted Christ. If I had a choice to call on Bill with little church background but who had come to church the last two Sundays or John who was faithful in the church every Sunday for 10 years but had not come at all for the last 4 years, I would call on Bill. Bill is moving toward God. John is moving or has moved away.

A Way to Understand Readiness

In *The Art of Sharing Your Faith* I have written,

> James Engel and Wilbert Norton helped me understand the importance of prospect receptivity in the development of their Spiritual Decision Process Model.[3] In that model, individuals are ranked based upon their knowledge, interest in, or response to the gospel. A person who has passed through the state of "initial awareness of the gospel" to a "positive attitude toward the gospel" is a better prospect for receiving Christ than the person who still is only at the "initial awareness of the gospel" stage. An individual at the "personal problem recognition" stage is even more likely to receive Christ than the individual at "positive attitude toward the gospel." The one with "personal problem recognition" has not only understood the gospel and come to like the gospel but now has a strong felt need for change. Because of this combination of factors, this person is most likely to accept Christ.[4]

Study my adaptation of the model on the next page. "Personal problem recognition" people have often gone through an insecurity-producing situation. Where would the prospects you listed at the end of chapter 1 fit on this chart?

SPIRITUAL DECISION PROCESS MODEL

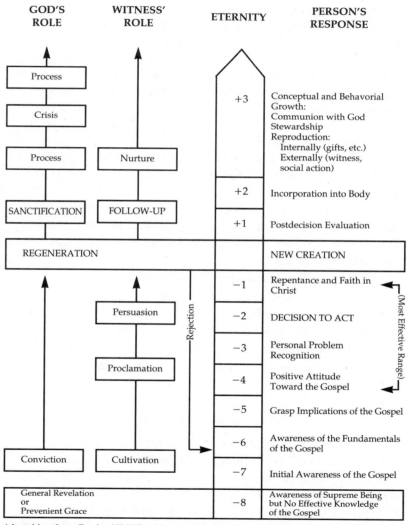

GOD'S ROLE	WITNESS' ROLE	ETERNITY	PERSON'S RESPONSE
Process		+3	Conceptual and Behavorial Growth: Communion with God Stewardship Reproduction: Internally (gifts, etc.) Externally (witness, social action)
Crisis			
Process	Nurture		
SANCTIFICATION	FOLLOW-UP	+2	Incorporation into Body
		+1	Postdecision Evaluation
REGENERATION			NEW CREATION
		−1	Repentance and Faith in Christ
	Persuasion	−2	DECISION TO ACT
		−3	Personal Problem Recognition
	Proclamation	−4	Positive Attitude Toward the Gospel
		−5	Grasp Implications of the Gospel
		−6	Awareness of the Fundamentals of the Gospel
Conviction	Cultivation	−7	Initial Awareness of the Gospel
General Revelation or Prevenient Grace		−8	Awareness of Supreme Being but No Effective Knowledge of the Gospel

Rejection

(Most Effective Range)

Adapted from James Engel and H. Wilbert Norton, *What's Gone Wrong with the Harvest?* p. 45. © 1975. Zondervan Corporation. Used by permission.

We also say of prospects, "The more natural, the better." When Rev. Dallas Mucci was considering the acceptance of a pastorate in Greater Pittsburgh, he asked the board members if they would take him to lunch with their business associates. They agreed, Mucci accepted the pastorate, and the board members invited him and their friends to lunch. Rev. Mucci had the privilege of seeing numbers of those contacts come to Christ and become active in the church because he was following natural channels. It is far more difficult to see the same results with "cold turkey" door-to-door calling. However, door-to-door calling will produce some results. It should not be despised, especially if the church has no other leads or prospects.

James Kennedy's *Evangelism Explosion* has had a major influence in our world in promoting witness and personal evangelism. Dr. Kennedy suggests an order of prospects with best prospects listed first:

1. People who have visited our services
2. Relatives and friends of new believers
3. Parents of children who have attended Sunday School (if Sunday School teachers have visited in the home)
4. Those who have bought new homes in the area.[5]

This listing confirms the principle: the more natural, the better.

Sowing and Reaping

If we depend mainly on pastors and evangelists for evangelism, there will be little or no growth of the Kingdom. On the other hand, if the great army of the laity can be mobilized, growth will be explosive. Witnessing laymen will strengthen the pulpit, because many people will not believe the preaching of the pulpit until it is backed up by the testimony of the pew. Public testimony, both planned and spontaneous, is a powerful tool for drawing people to Christ. Some will not even make their first step into the church until personal witness has paved the way. My mother had been living a godless life for more than 25 years. When I came home the Christmas following my conversion to tell her I had found Jesus, she developed a strange hunger for God. She moved from twice-a-year church attendance to regular attendance at a Nazarene church. In a revival under a Nazarene evangelist, she was saved. Today she is a radiant Christian, but the awakening in her and the subsequent church attendance happened only after personal witness. I had the privilege of sowing. The evangelist had the privilege of reaping.

Notice the language of Jesus in John 4:34-38. The field is ripe for harvest. To harvest when the crop is ready is important; timing is of the essence. We do not want to harvest too early—when the crop is not yet developed or the fruit is green. On the other hand, we do not want to wait so long we lose the crop. When Cambodian refugees began to move to our area, and a few began to visit our church, we knew we had about one year's time to reach them with the gospel. After a year, they would be infected with materialism, their openness would turn to guardedness, and the harvest would be lost. We established an English as a second language Sunday School class for Cambodians. Soon we were averaging more than 50 a Sunday in Cambodian attendance. Today these Cambodians have established their own church, which has a Cambodian pastor.

The language of John 4 stresses both sowing and reaping. Apparently the sower prepares the ground and plants the seed. The reaper harvests the results of the sower's efforts. Paul warns us not to become proud of what we do to produce harvest. In what I call the law of harvest, Paul says in 1 Cor.

3:6, "I planted the seed, Apollos watered it, but God made it grow." No pride over either planting or watering—because only God can make things grow (v. 7). Note that harnessing our pride does not remove our responsibility. Verse 9 goes on to say, "We are God's fellow workers."

In Matt. 9:35-38, Jesus has staked out a "Help Wanted" sign. He has studied the crowd with compassion; He has counted them as harvest. They should be gathered before the storm so that they are not lost. He asks His disciples to pray that the Lord will "send out workers into his harvest field" (v. 38). In the next chapter, we see that the ones who prayed are the same ones who are sent. With William McCumber we say, "Without exalting man or belittling God, we insist that Jesus needs help to gather His harvest."[6]

It is important that our harvesting flow from compassion. Jesus had compassion on the multitudes. He was concerned about their sickness (Matt. 14:14), demon oppression (Mark 9:22), sorrow (Luke 7:13), hunger (Matt. 15:32), loneliness (Mark 1:41). Yet most supremely He was concerned because they were common people desperately longing for God.

William Barclay describes the scene:

> The Pharisees saw the common people as chaff to be destroyed and burned up; Jesus saw them as a harvest to be reaped and to be saved. The Pharisees in their pride looked for the destruction of sinners; Jesus in love died for the salvation of sinners ... The harvest will never be reaped unless there are reapers to reap it ... *Jesus Christ needs men* ... He was never outside Palestine, and there was a world which was waiting ... It is the dream of Christ that every man should be a ... reaper.[7]

Someone you know needs Jesus now!

When a Christian establishes a friendship with a non-Christian, the Christian is sowing seeds and cultivating soil. People are more apt to become Christians if they already have

Christian friends. People are more apt to stay Christians if they have Christian friends.

In John 4:38, Jesus teaches that the reapers reaped what they did not work for. The sowers did the hard work. But Jesus is not saying that harvesting is an easy task. Sowing requires more patience, love, and plain inconvenience—with less visible results. And though harvesting does not entail the long-range work, it is intentional and intensive action. When the harvest is standing ripe in the fields, a breakdown in equipment or shortage of laborers does not cause the farmer to casually say, "Oh, I'll wait till next year." No! The nature of the harvest demands that we get the job done now. Let's face it—both sowing and reaping are hard work. Remember it in discouraging days. Paul had to remind his people, "Let us not become weary in doing good, for at the proper time we will reap a harvest if we do not give up" (Gal. 6:9).

Sometimes we are tempted to honor the reapers and forget the sowers. Jesus said, "Even now the reaper . . . harvests the crop for eternal life, so that *the sower and the reaper may be glad together*" (John 4:36, italics mine).

In 1986 Dr. Bruce Taylor was sent to Nigeria to salvage and strengthen a fledgling Church of the Nazarene in that country. The individual and group he was sent to help did not seem cooperative. In the midst of Dr. Taylor's frustrated efforts, another group and leader emerged. It seems that during World War II, Nigerians serving in that cause met some Nazarene servicemen. These servicemen witnessed and left literature with a spiritual message with these Nigerians. The Nigerians took the literature home, were impressed by what they read, and sensed an identity with the message of the Church of the Nazarene. They discovered an address of the publishing house on the literature. They wrote and got a *Manual* explaining the beliefs, practices, and policy of the church. In

1946 they established the Church of the Nazarene in Nigeria on their own. On Easter 1987 Dr. Taylor and Rev. John Seaman had the privilege of receiving 40 churches and 6,500 Nigerian members officially into the international Church of the Nazarene.[8] And all of this was because some solider boys sowed some seed many years before. A little seed can go a long way.

For several years now I have been talking about three groups of workers in the church. These are cultivators, converters, and conservers. The cultivator is the sower of seed. He or she may have the gift of hospitality and knows how to build bridges of friendship to the unsaved. This person witnesses. The converter may have the gift of evangelism and deals with people in intensive face-to-face encounter and leads them to Christ. Not only are the facts of the gospel presented, but there is a call to decision. This person may be called soul winner, reaper, personal evangelist, or harvester. The conserver may have gifts of exhortation, encouragement, pastor, or teacher. A special concern for people equips the conserver to follow up and establish new Christians in their faith.

Because of spiritual gifts, we may find ourselves most comfortable spending much of our ministry in one particular realm. Yet we must not allow the teaching about gifts to become an excuse for spiritual irresponsibility. You would not accept the argument, "I don't have the gift of liberality, so I won't tithe." You wouldn't contend: "I don't have the gift of intercession, so I won't pray." Likewise, we cannot say, "I don't have the gift of evangelist, so I won't witness." All Christians are expected to tithe, pray, and witness. Witness was the pattern of New Testament laity. The calls of Christ to witness are to all Christians.

However, let's not forget that any part a person plays in

bringing someone to Christ is a good thing. There is a lot of glory in harvest, but no one can harvest unless many people sow. Jesus said, "The sower and the reaper may be glad together" (John 4:36). Those involved in the early witness that starts a person to Christ and those involved in the final witness just before conversion are both valuable.

Edna and Don

Janet had been raised in a nominal church but had no evangelical understanding. Now for several years she had not attended at all. In the apartment above her, Edna came in to do housekeeping for an elderly man. Edna, the housekeeper, loved Jesus, talked about her joyous relationship with Christ, and told Janet Jesus loved her too. Edna invited Janet to come with her to her church, the Church of the Nazarene. Janet's heart was warmed by the services. Then suddenly Edna died. Upset, Janet quit church for a while.

Sometime later Janet married Mike. They moved to a new home. With new marriage and new home, Janet felt the need to make a new beginning spiritually. She remembered her good experience at Edna's church and searched the Saturday newspaper for the nearest Nazarene church. Janet and Mike visited the church.

In a short time, Don, of the congregation Janet and Mike visited, phoned and talked with Mike and Janet. Don suggested that he might stop by to visit with them, get to know them better, and tell them some more about the church. Don also said he'd like to bring a couple of other folks from the church. Mike and Janet liked the idea. On March 25, a Thursday night, Don took Paula and Robert to visit Mike and Janet. Their discussion eventually turned to Jesus. The Holy Spirit was there, and Janet was ready. She invited Christ into her life and was transformed. As a result of the call of Don and the call of the Lord, Mike renewed a long-broken relationship with Christ.[9]

Who should get the credit—Edna who sowed the seed, or Don who reaped the harvest? Both should rejoice—they were used by God. But God should get the glory (1 Cor. 3:6-7). Today Mike and Janet are leaders in their local church, Don and Paula are missionaries in Africa, Robert is pastoring a fast-growing church on the west coast of the United States, and Edna, the housekeeper, is in the presence of the Lord.

Whenever you help one person to come one step closer to Christ, you have pleased God. You may be the witness who leads that prospect to Christ, or you may be the witness who plants the seed. Any progress up the spiritual decision process model is good and to the glory of God.

Understandable Language

Paul the apostle was deeply concerned about how to identify with the people to whom he witnessed and preached. He wanted them to understand his message. He carefully considered their culture and station in life. Listen to him:

> Though I am free and belong to no man, I make myself a slave to everyone, to win as many as possible. To the Jews I became like a Jew, to win the Jews. . . . I have become all things to all men so that by all possible means I might save some (1 Cor. 9:19-20, 22).

When you analyze Paul's synagogue preaching, as in Pisidian Antioch (Acts 13:13-43), he speaks in the language a well-trained Jew would understand. He draws heavily on Old Testament promise. His audience is called to find forgiveness in Jesus and believe in Christ. However, when the same Paul preaches to the philosophers at the Areopagus in idol-filled Athens, his message draws, not on the Old Testament, but on their familiar idols of worship and Greek poets to point them to repentance and Christ (17:22-34). Friedrich says, "The New Testament speaks the language of its day."[10] So should we. How will the gospel speak to present-day hopes and human needs?

James Kennedy urges us to avoid misunderstood words in our witness. Many terms precious to us are not understood by the world—words and phrases like "saved," "regenerated," "sanctified," "Amen," and "Praise God!" We need to take the truths of these words and put them in a form understood by the person to whom we speak.[11] Think about your witness. Is it understandable to its hearers?

Every Christmas, our local church asks a new Christian to give a witness in church, emphasizing how Christmas has become different with Christ. One year we asked Dan Durick, who is an executive in the restaurant industry. Prayerfully he prepared his testimony. Our congregation is reaching many businesspeople and professionals and includes those who consider themselves "moving up." Dan used some of the language of the church—words like "saved" and "sanctified" —but he surrounded them with so much of the language that the aggressive business and professional young adults of our congregation would understand that his message made a powerful impact. When the service was over, people crowded around Dan to talk further. Among them were those who were attending their very first service in our church. Let this testimony speak to you at the same time you sense how it would be understood by its hearers.

I was raised in the church.
I was a church "brat," the son of an active Sunday School teacher and church lover.
I was friends with, and used to play with, the pastor's kids.
I was mentally saved, on Sunday night, November 11, 1956, at

age 9 because when you are a kid in the church, it was the thing to do.

I was baptized (by immersion) in 1963, at age 16.

I left home to attend chef's school in Connecticut in September 1965.

Free at last—no one to answer to,
except me, of course.
Free to live my way,
free to make my own decisions—
on everything . . . hurrrrray!
If I wanted to go to class, I could (and did!).
If I wanted to eat lunch at 11:30—or 2:30—I could.
If I wanted to party all night, and play all day, I could.
If I wanted to smoke, I could.
If I wanted to go to church, I could (and didn't!).
I was in control! There was no one I had to answer to.
For the next 24 *years,* I *was*
(or better stated, Satan was) in control of my life.

All of my life—
my personal life,
my professional life,
my financial life.
I'm sure you understand there was just "no time" for spiritual life; I was too busy climbing the corporate ladder.

Corporate life—
where you are taught that to be powerful, you must be *emotionless. Insensitive.*
You are taught to be *self-sufficient* and *goal-oriented.*
The company first,
yourself second,
and should you so choose, family third.
God and business just don't mix;
you can just forget about Sundays off.
Get over those religious sensitivities, mister.

We're going to make something out of you.
Don't worry! Be happy—or at least look happy!

Ah, corporate life, where you are taught that you are, and must be, *always* right, even when you are wrong—even at the expense of other people. "It's them or us!"
Your *only* measure of achievement and success is the size of your paycheck.
Your only competition is at the bank teller's window.
The more you make, the better job you did.
And so for many, many years of my life, I was working on my career.
I became an industry leader.
I had it made.

Then *I* decided to change my life.
In March of 1987, after 21 years of smoking three and a half packs of cigarettes a day, I suddenly decided,
for no apparent reason,
I wanted to stop smoking.
Being self-dependent and self-assured, I stopped smoking cold turkey, without any form of withdrawal, without any further desires. I was tough. I did the impossible.
Do you really believe *I* was in control of that?

I had achieved the highest food and beverage position in the United States, in control of the largest number of fine dining, white tablecloth and dinner house restaurants in America.
Highest in position stature . . .
and second highest in salary in the restaurant industry.
Oh, how much California "good-life" life-style money can buy!

In 1989 *I* even decided to be benevolent.
I decided to take over a $100,000-a-year *cut* in salary and return to Kansas City to work for, and help, my former boss (one of the men that "made" me) with his recently acquired, and un-

fortunately faltering, business enterprise.
Just to show I really did have the capacity to care.

And, as a further display of benevolence,
and to appease my wonderful mother,
Sunday, November 19, 1989,
we for the first time visited Kansas City First Church,
at the recommendation of a lifelong Nazarene friend,
a friend of Mother's from Pittsburgh.

After my politically oriented, meaningless attendances at the likes of California's Crystal Cathedral and New York's St. Patrick's Cathedral, churches where, for *good* business reasons, I needed to "be seen," I'm sure you can imagine how very impressed I was with First Church's "sanctinasium" facility.
But, oh, well, *I* knew that after the holidays I could return to good, old First United Mattress for my Sunday morning "rejuvenation."
After all, I was still in control!

Or thought I was in control,
until the Sunday morning service on December 31, when we sang "Majesty." Something happened. I felt different . . .
I didn't know what it was.
It ran a chill through me.
Tears filled my eyes.
Understand, please, these were sensations I had never experienced before.
This was a new experience.
It made me come back,
even after Mother went back home.
It was something that made me curious.

It made me buy a Bible (the King James Version).
It made me buy another Bible (the NIV)
so that I could understand what Pastor Wright was saying to me—"*to me?*" . . .

Hey, what's going on here?
Oh, thank *God* for the powerful workings of the Holy Spirit.
Well, I continued to worship and learn in this church.
I didn't realize it then, but I was under conviction by the Holy Spirit.
I didn't resist . . . I don't know why . . . I just couldn't.

On Sunday, February 18, 1990, during the announcement of the success of the sanctuary fund-raising campaign, *I was reclaimed by the blood of the Lord Jesus Christ, my Savior!*

And on Saturday, March 3, during the membership class with Pastors Wright and Shaver,
at the invitation of Pastor Wright, I was sanctified wholly by the Lord God Almighty.
Oh, what glory! . . .

"But whatever *was* to my profit
I *now* consider *loss*
for the sake of *Christ*.

What is more,
I consider *everything* a *loss*
compared to the *surpassing greatness*
of *knowing* Christ Jesus
my Lord,
for whose sake I have lost *all things*.

I consider them *rubbish,*
that *I* may gain *Christ*."

(Paul's letter to the Philippians while in prison, 3:7 and 8, italics added)

This week, let's remember:
Christ was born on Christmas;
He is alive today.

He *is not* just for children;
He *is not* just for Christmas.

He *is* for each and every one of us—
not just for the holiday,
but for every hour of every day.
This year, join me in putting *Christ* back into Christmas.

This story is more than just a Christmas celebration—more than the celebration of Jesus Christ's birth. The gift goes on!
Forgiveness of sins, through the blood of the Lamb of God, the Lord Jesus Christ; redemption, salvation, reclamation, and sanctification through God's mighty power and grace; daily guidance, direction, and care from this precious Holy Spirit.
I am so thankful *this* Christmas, Christmas 1990, that I have received these gifts of God.
"For by *grace* are ye saved through *faith;* and that not of yourselves: it is the gift *of God:* not of works, lest any man should boast" (Eph. 2:8 and 9, KJV, italics added).[12]

Webs

The Bible says that Jesus is the Light (John 1:5). What role did John the Baptist play in Christ's ministry? Verse 7 says, "He came as a witness to testify concerning that light, so that through him all men might believe." Consider John 1:35-46:

[35]The next day John was there again with two of his disciples. [36]When he saw Jesus passing by, he said, "Look, the Lamb of God!"

[37]When the two disciples heard him say this, they followed Jesus. [38]Turning around, Jesus saw them following and asked, "What do you want?"

They said, "Rabbi" (which means Teacher), "where are you staying?"

[39]"Come," he replied, "and you will see."

So they went and saw where he was staying, and spent that day with him. It was about the tenth hour.

[40]Andrew, Simon Peter's brother, was one of the two who heard what John had said and who had followed Jesus. [41]The

first thing Andrew did was to find his brother Simon and tell him, "We have found the Messiah" (that is, the Christ). ⁴²And he brought him to Jesus.

Jesus looked at him and said, "You are Simon son of John. You will be called Cephas" (which, when translated, is Peter).

⁴³The next day Jesus decided to leave for Galilee. Finding Philip, he said to him, "Follow me."

⁴⁴Philip, like Andrew and Peter, was from the town of Bethsaida. ⁴⁵Philip found Nathanael and told him, "We have found the one Moses wrote about in the Law, and about whom the prophets also wrote—Jesus of Nazareth, the son of Joseph."

⁴⁶"Nazareth! Can anything good come from there?" Nathanael asked.

"Come and see," said Philip.

John wants us to know the importance of personal witness in the outreach of the church. So in chapter 1 he gives us the pattern. From the moment we discover the truth about Jesus, we are constrained to pass it on. This is to be a pattern for all Christians.

Note in John 1:41 Andrew finds his brother Peter to tell him about Jesus. It's natural to go to our own kin first, our best prospects, the ones with whom we already have the best understanding. Next Philip responds to Christ. Like Andrew and Peter, he's from Bethsaida. One wonders if Andrew and Peter had prepared him. Philip is excited enough to pass the message to Nathanael.

Under Paul's ministry the jailer comes to Christ. The next ones to be converted are—naturally—his own household (Acts 16:31-34). Family evangelism is common in the New Testament, especially in Acts. In 10:24, Cornelius "had called together his relatives and close friends" to hear the gospel. Then, 18:8 tells us Crispus, the synagogue ruler, saw his household come to Christ. And homes become centers of the gospel's spread—Jason in Thessalonica (17:5), Lydia in Philippi (16:15), and Priscilla and Aquila in Rome, Corinth, and Ephesus (18:1-2, 19, 26).

Today the above description of the spread of the gospel is called web evangelism. Win and Charles Arn say, "Webs of common kinship (the larger family), common friendship (friends and neighbors) and common associates (special interests, work relationship, and recreation) are still the paths most people follow in becoming Christian today."[13] Philippines pastor Vern Tamayo said to me, "A grandfather is a times 10." He meant that if you win the grandfather to Christ, that is 10 times greater than winning another member of the family because the grandfather has influence and will evangelize the children and grandchildren. However, we did see the children influencing their parents to come to Christ while we were in the Philippines. Webs were working.

The Institute of American Church Growth surveyed 14,000 laity with this question, "What or who was responsible for your coming to Christ and your church?" Seventy-five to 90 percent said it was because a friend or relative influenced them.[14] The average church member has eight friends and relatives outside Christ and the church.[15] A couple in Grove City, Ohio, found Christ and began to witness to their friends. "The Family Tree" was the result, bringing 35 adults and 32 children to Christ and the church. See the illustration of this on the next page.

Sometimes family members will be resistant. Jesus' family opposed Him (Matt. 12:46-50). In Mark 3:21 we discover His brothers thought Him mad. Later the New Testament writers give us encouragement. By Acts 12:17 and 21:18 Jesus' brother James is leader of the Jerusalem church. He authors the Book of James. Take courage!

In the summer of 1989 my wife and I were invited to hold revival services in Watertown and LaFargeville, N.Y.,

The Evangelism Family Tree

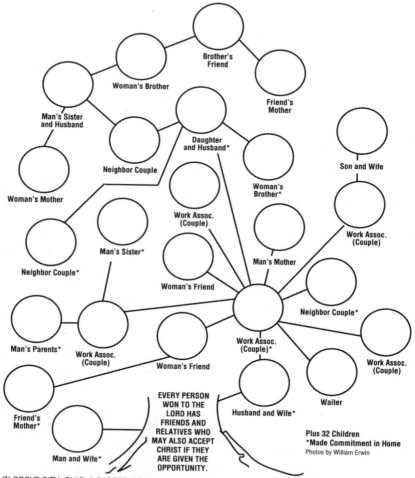

Brother's Friend

Woman's Brother

Friend's Mother

Man's Sister and Husband

Daughter and Husband*

Woman's Mother

Neighbor Couple

Son and Wife

Woman's Brother*

Work Assoc. (Couple)

Work Assoc. (Couple)

Man's Sister*

Neighbor Couple*

Man's Mother

Woman's Friend

Neighbor Couple*

Man's Parents*

Work Assoc. (Couple)

Woman's Friend

Work Assoc. (Couple)*

Work Assoc. (Couple)

Waiter

Friend's Mother*

EVERY PERSON WON TO THE LORD HAS FRIENDS AND RELATIVES WHO MAY ALSO ACCEPT CHRIST IF THEY ARE GIVEN THE OPPORTUNITY.

Husband and Wife*

Plus 32 Children
*Made Commitment in Home
Photos by William Erwin

Man and Wife*

IN GROVE CITY, OHIO, A PASTOR WON A YOUNG COUPLE TO CHRIST, AND AS A RESULT 35 OTHER PEOPLE (PLUS 32 CHILDREN) CAME TO KNOW CHRIST AND ARE ACTIVE IN THE CHURCH. FROM ONE SEED OF FAITH HAS GROWN A GREAT TREE OF BELIEVERS. AN AGGRESSIVE PROGRAM OF PERSONAL EVANGELISM CAN PRODUCE A FOREST OF FAITH IN CHURCHES EVERYWHERE.

For more information write: Church of the Nazarene, EVANGELISM MINISTRIES
6401 The Paseo, Kansas City, MO 64131, Toll-free WATS line 800-821-2154

area. My Aunt Mary had accepted Christ through my mother's witness and joined the Church of the Nazarene. I had many blood relatives in the area. With Aunt Mary's help, I wrote letters to 125 blood relatives. I had some significant conversations with loved ones there. Thirty-four of my loved ones came out to revival services. Twelve came forward for prayer and to seek God.

*　　*　　*

Your Response

You have been praying for five people who need Jesus now. You have been reporting to a Christian friend about your own spiritual growth. Now based on what you've learned about who is ready, list your prospects in the order of most responsive first.

PROSPECTS IN ORDER OF RESPONSIVENESS

1. _____

2. _____

3. _____

4. _____

5. _____

Next invite at least one of your prospects to come to church with you next Sunday. You might include an invitation to a meal as part of your church invitation. Think through ahead of time how you'll express yourself. To a close friend or neighbor you might say,

> Jack and Jeanne, you've been our good neighbors and are among our best friends. We want you to know what it means to us to have friends like you. We'd like you to be our guests at our

church this Sunday. Afterward we'd like to have you to our house for dinner. We are proud of you as our friends, and we are proud of our pastor and church friends. We'd be so glad if you could meet each other.[16]

If they already have a commitment this Sunday, you might follow with, "What about doing this your first available Sunday?"

Share the result of your invitation with a trusted Christian friend. Or if you are part of a class studying this book, share with the class. Endeavor to share what might be most encouraging to them.

4

Overcoming the Fear Factor

Oswald Chambers said,

> We have the notion that we can consecrate our gifts to God. You cannot consecrate what is not yours; there is only one thing you can consecrate to God, and that is the right to yourself (Romans 12:1). If you will give God your right to yourself, He will make a holy experiment out of you.[1]

A *holy experiment!* I don't know about you, but those words intrigue me. Wouldn't it be a challenge to let God take you beyond what you've ever experienced before in effective witness? Say to yourself, "Today God's holy experiment starts in me!"

My Hands Sweat, My Mouth Is Dry

I have shared what Jesus means to me hundreds of times. I have regularly gone out to visit people and had the privilege of sharing the gospel with them. Many of these people have accepted Christ and today are active in the church. Yet to this day, when I go out on a call with the goal of sharing Christ, my hands sweat and my mouth gets dry. I have come to accept a certain amount of nervousness as normal. Increasingly I am convinced that fear is the silent robber of our effectiveness both in witness and soul winning. There is a tremendous resistance to personal witness and personal evangelism by many Christians. If they would search deep down, I think they would discover the root is subconscious fear. Remember, you are doing a most loving thing when you offer Christ to a friend. But there is danger your friend might misunderstand, and you will offend him or her. We all fear offending people. Yet, as Richard Peace puts it, "If our intention to be faithful witnesses to Christ is serious, then we must confront and conquer our fear."[2]

Peter—Before and After

It is important to realize that fear may produce either a sinful or a truly human and legitimate response. Look at Peter in Mark 14:66-71. He is afraid to be associated with Jesus, because Jesus is very unpopular at the moment. Jesus is headed toward the Cross, and it's anybody's guess what might happen to those who identify with Christ. When a servant girl asks him about his association with Jesus, Peter denied knowing Christ. His decision and response in this fear-filled situation was sinful.

Something changed Peter. In Acts 4:1-13, he faces great fear-producing circumstances. He has been preaching Jesus. He is arrested and imprisoned for it. Then he faces a harsh grilling by the authorities. Now notice his decision and response: "Then Peter, filled with the Holy Spirit, said to them . . ." (v. 8), and there follows his courageous speech for Christ. His courage is great enough to be noticed (v. 13). Peter was different because he'd been filled with the Spirit (2:4). The fullness of the Spirit is the major source of sufficient courage to witness.

It is not enough to leave it there. The disciples are called before the Sanhedrin again, threatened, and dismissed. The account continues in chapter 4:

²³On their release, Peter and John went back to their own people and reported all that the chief priests and elders had said to them. ²⁴When they heard this, they raised their voices together in prayer to God. "Sovereign Lord," they said, "you made the heaven and the earth and the sea, and everything in them. ²⁵You spoke by the Holy Spirit through the mouth of your servant, our father David:

> " 'Why do the nations rage and the peoples plot in vain?
> ²⁶The kings of the earth take their stand and the rulers gather together against the Lord and against his Anointed One.'
>
> ²⁷Indeed Herod and Pontius Pilate met together with the Gentiles and the people of Israel in this city to conspire against your holy servant Jesus, whom you anointed. ²⁸They did what your power and will had decided beforehand should happen. ²⁹Now, Lord, consider their threats and enable your servants to speak your word with great boldness. ³⁰Stretch out your hand to heal and perform miraculous signs and wonders through the name of your holy servant Jesus."

³¹After they prayed, the place where they were meeting was shaken. And they were all filled with the Holy Spirit and spoke the word of God boldly.

Obviously Peter experiences a sense of fear again. He and others pray that the Lord will "consider their threats" (v. 29). The disciples' great concern is not self-preservation but that God will "enable your servants to speak your word with great boldness" (v. 29). God's answer was a fresh infilling of the Holy Spirit and its result—again, bold speech (v. 31).

In all three cases, Peter experiences fear. In all three cases, Peter is in danger. In all three cases he decides what he will say about Christ. In the first case he denies Him. In the next two, he speaks boldly for Him. The difference is the power of the Spirit. It is necessary for even the Spirit-filled

Christian of 4:8 to have fresh infillings of the Spirit (v. 31) in order to have sufficient courage for new challenges. No wonder we have talked of witness out of the overflow. Realistically we admit that even a Spirit-filled Christian may feel fear in a new pressure and may need to pray afresh—and be filled afresh.

New Testament Courage

Early in my Christian life, I thought that it was the state of the Spirit-filled Christian to be free from the feeling of fear. Then one day I read the testimony of the Spirit-filled apostle Paul: "I came to you in weakness and fear, and with much trembling" (1 Cor. 2:3). In the very next verse he says his message came "with a demonstration of the Spirit's power." *Paul felt fear,* even as a Spirit-empowered person. As a result, I have a new definition of courage. New Testament courage is not the absence of the feeling of fear. It is the willingness to do what God wants you to do, even though you have the feeling of fear.

There are a number of sources for our fear. We may feel we will fail because someone will say no to our witness. Did Jesus fail in His witness? Did He fail when the rich young ruler refused to put God first? Did He fail because one of the thieves on the cross failed to acknowledge Him as Lord? These facts have led Bill Bright to the conclusion: "The ministry of Jesus Christ modeled for us a liberating truth about our witnessing efforts: *Success in witnessing is simply taking the initiative to share Christ in the power of the Holy Spirit, and leaving the results to God.*"[3]

Keith Wright has made some helpful observations about this fear issue. We may fear we don't know Scripture well enough. He reminds us Jesus used fishermen. We may fear

71

questions will be raised that we cannot answer. He suggests we ask permission to return later with the answer. We may fear sharing the gospel prematurely. He reminds us that most people need to hear the gospel several times before they respond. Admitting fear is rational because most people experience it, Rev. Wright says that our love for Christ must be greater than the fear that keeps us from sharing God's love.[4]

Probably most of us will work through our fears about witnessing by a series of progressive steps. God is pleased if we can make a step of progress even if we haven't reached the final goal. I'll review the stages I've gone through in more than 35 years of sharing my Savior.

1. As a new Christian, I was anxious to tell people what Jesus did for me. I talked to many people. Only a few ever accepted Christ.

2. About six years into my first pastorate, I took a one-week course in Campus Crusade training and learned how to present the "Four Spiritual Laws." This was helpful to me because it gave me a structure for presenting basic truths to people. However, for the last day of the seminar, they asked us to go calling and present the gospel. I told them I was too busy with my sermon preparation for that Sunday (which was true). This was my conscious reason. Now I realize my subconscious reason was my fear.

3. A few days later, Hal came to see me in my office. He and his family had recently begun coming to our church. He told me there was something wrong in his life. He felt guilty. He had no purpose. He wasn't happy. Did I know what was wrong? I used my new training and shared the "Four Spiritual Laws" with Hal. He repented, accepted Christ, and was changed. His wife and children accepted Christ. Hal and his wife joined the church. My confidence soared! It worked!

4. I began to witness with the "Four Laws" being my

structure to present the basic faith of the gospel. I saw others accept Christ.

5. After nine years pastoring that first church, I entered the field of full-time evangelism. While in a revival with Rev. Dale Galloway, he took me door-to-door calling. I was amazed to see how responsive people were to a warm and relaxed approach. This was primarily friendship calling. At the end of the first day, Rev. Galloway said, "We're going to do this again tomorrow. Only you'll do the talking at the door." I went home terrified. I prayed. I felt God wanted me to do it despite my fears. The next day I led the calls, and people were responsive again. My confidence moved up another notch.

6. Two and a half years later I was starting an assignment teaching evangelism at Nazarene Theological Seminary. Dr. James Kennedy had just spoken at a conference on evangelism in Kansas City. Some of our other seminary professors, hearing him, thought it would be good for me to attend his personal evangelism school. In a few days I received an invitation to Dr. Kennedy's school in Florida. That night as I prayed, I was gripped by that old fear: I was comfortable with a "Four Laws" approach, I had just started to teach, I didn't know if I could handle more change just now. Yet—despite the negative feelings, I was sure God wanted me to go. It was an extraordinary experience. I came home convinced the Kennedy *Evangelism Explosion* approach would make me a better witness.

7. I enthusiastically announced to my seminary classes the results of my experiences at Kennedy's school. I offered to go calling with any student who had a prospect. That Friday I was leading a call, and I saw people praying to receive Christ. Another defeat of my fear.

8. Now I am regularly sharing my witness, offering

Christ and His plan of salvation to people, and seeing them accept Christ.

I have come to believe 2 Tim. 1:7, "For God did not give us a spirit of timidity, but a spirit of power, of love and of self-discipline." Despite continuing experiences of wet hands and dry mouth, God's Spirit of power predominates. Have you battled fear as I have? Would you let God lead you past your present fear to the next stage on your journey of courage for the cause of Christ's witness?

Try Friendship Evangelism

When we studied the witnessing of Andrew and Philip to Peter and Nathanael in John 1, you may have noticed something. Andrew and Philip gave a simple witness and brought their prospect to Jesus. Jesus did the intensive work and called them to commitment. It may be best to think of Andrew and Philip as doing witness and friendship evangelism rather than personal evangelism. That could be a starting place for you too.

Friendship evangelism teaches Christians to build bridges of love and friendship with non-Christians. The friendship is built on a common need or common interest. Both the Christian and non-Christian may be interested in sports, and that common area becomes the basis of friendship. That's why a church softball team can become an evangelistic tool. Other common interests can be crafts, business interests, children, service clubs. From the friendship, we introduce the non-Christian to the church and other Christians. It may be another Christian who will call them to decision for Christ. Friendship evangelism is less threatening than personal evangelism, and many more Christians will be able to do it. Learning to build these bridges of friendship with non-Christians is important, because we tend to have fewer non-Christian friends the longer we are in the church.

Observe the friendship evangelism in this report: David has been serving as a civil engineer in the country of Kuwait. He'd established his home there with his wife, Linda, and their children, Charles, age 11, and Sarah, age 9. And, as far as we know, David and Linda and Charles and Sarah were the only Nazarenes who had been living in Kuwait. When Saddam Hussein's Iraqi troops invaded Kuwait on August 2, 1990, we were concerned about David and Linda.

How did David ever become a part of the Church of the Nazarene? A graduate of the University of Rhode Island, he came to work as a young engineer for Black and Veatch in Kansas City. As he was driving one day, he spied a group of teenagers on a church parking lot washing cars. He pulled in to have his car washed, and he was so impressed with their warmth and friendliness that when they said to him, "David, why don't you visit our church this Sunday?" he came to the worship service at First Church of the Nazarene. That was the first time he had ever been in a Nazarene church. The first call I made as a member of the staff at Kansas City First Church was to David. I discovered that he had come to know the Lord in college through a Christian group on campus. David had a lot of questions, so I found a young seminary student who was willing to meet with David every week and lead him through the *Basic Bible Studies*. David eventually joined this church as a new Nazarene.[5]

I am happy to report that at the time of the invasion, David and his family were vacationing in the United States and were spared the tragedies of the war. Although the ministry of the church to David was not directly winning an unsaved person to Christ, the dynamics were the same. The common interest between the teens and David was cars. They exercised friendship and invited him. I was the one God used for the more direct encounter dealing with his present relationship with God. Friendship evangelism at work!

Hurdling Social Barriers

Many Christians are afraid to witness because they don't know how to handle the social barriers between themselves and non-Christians. These are real. For example, in the United States culture, you can't say to the unsaved person, "Come to a party," and expect them to understand. In the secular realm, "party" connotes a gathering with alcoholic beverages. Biblically we are called to maintain a separation from the world (James 1:27 and 4:4), and yet we are exhorted to love, evangelize, and win the ungodly. The implications of the call of Jesus to be fishers of men (Mark 1:17) is that to catch fish, you have to go to where the fish are. Jesus models this for us, as in His association with tax collectors and sinners at Matthew's home (Matt. 9:9-13). It would be shocking to ever think Jesus would get drunk, become involved in sexual immorality, tell dirty stories, or cheat someone out of his or her hard-earned cash—yet He evangelized those who did. He saw them as sick people who needed a doctor.

I have discovered ways to deal with these social barriers. When I am inviting a non-Christian into a social setting, I give a *clear, specific* invitation. It is *not*, "Come to a party at my house." That is a misunderstood signal. It's, "Come to our place Saturday for hamburgers on the grill. Then we'd like you to be our guests at the ball game. The Royals play the Red Sox." Or, "Please come with us to church Sunday night. After service we'd like you and some of our friends from church to come to our place for refreshments. We'd be proud for our church friends to meet you." You notice how this invitation gives them a clear understanding of what will happen. They won't feel tricked, and knowing what to expect reduces their fear.

Another help for me in this "social barrier" issue is that I keep control of the situation. Let me illustrate. Our neighbors invited us to their Christmas party. We had seen the party the previous year. About 20 guests left very intoxicated. My main job the next day was picking up their liquor bottles from my lawn. My wife and I did not think we could do much good for the cause of Christ at their party—their turf, their friends, their agenda, their liquor. It would be 18 drunks and two sober Nazarenes.[6]

Yet our response to their invitation was important. We are not to condemn. "Bill and Mary," I said, "thanks for asking us. We're not able to come, but let's get together another time."

The next year my wife and I planned an "International Christmas Party." I invited international students from Nazarene Theological Seminary, Kansas City, where I teach, to come to the party. Each was asked to bring a food representing their country and be prepared to tell about Christmas customs in their country. I also asked for some students to weave a bit of personal testimony into the Christmas custom report. We invited neighbors and told them that seminary students were coming, so they would know the nature of the evening. That night our home was filled with unchurched people. They enjoyed exotic food and heard tales of Christmas in the Cape Verde Islands, Holland, Mexico, and elsewhere. When Cor Holleman reported on Holland, he skillfully wove his testimony into the report. Five years later, a guest of that evening, who had moved to another part of town, returned to tell of how she and her husband had recently received spiritual help. We believe the seed was sown the night of the International Party.

We have been laying down principles to help overcome social barriers and build bridges of friendship. So far we have discussed:

1. Give a clear invitation.
2. Keep control of the situation.
3. Contact others socially.
4. Establish a common interest.
5. Don't condemn.

Two other principles are:

6. Arouse interest.
7. Don't go too far.

"Arouse interest" means you choose some words that raise curiosity or interest in your hearer, then you continue speaking to those who respond. It means you are being salt to make people thirst for Christ. Christ intrigued the Samaritan woman into further questions by His comments in John 4:13. "Don't go too far" means we give only as much message as the prospect is ready for. Our tendency is to see a faint glimmer of interest and rush in with the whole story. By relying on the Holy Spirit, we can gain poise.[7]

"Don't go too far" protects our feelings as Christians. One person said to me that she was afraid to witness because people would make fun of her. However, if you only share as much as people are ready to hear, you may protect yourself as well as being effective with them. None of us likes to be made fun of. It will help us to remember, however, that though the sinner's way is the average, the Christian's way is normal. If someone chides you for being a Christian, try the casual approach. Ask your friend, "Have you ever really tried living the Christian life?" When he or she says, "Well, no," give a big smile and say, "Don't knock it till you try it!"

Opportunities and on Purpose

When Matthew was converted to Christ, he brought his pen with him from his tax books. God used this man of careful detail and organizational skills to write the story of Jesus. So we have Matthew's Gospel. Today God often uses the gifts and skills already developed in a person as a channel for witness. Bonnie Perry is a Christian by her commitment and a book editor by vocation. It is no surprise that God has used her and her sister-in-law, Judi, to write an inspirational novel, *A Season Till Spring.*[8] Charles Colson, former adviser to U.S. President Richard Nixon, was convicted for crimes and imprisoned. In the midst of his gathering troubles, Colson found Christ. God has given him a powerful witness to the political community and the prison population. Little wonder—God is using his past skills, contacts, and experiences. Ann Kiemel Anderson prays God will make her creative. When Ann is reaching out to Scott and his junior high friends in their boys' club, Scott's mother calls and asks permission to provide refreshments for the boys. What do you suppose Ann concludes? Now she has a chance to reach Scott's mom and dad. Creative! Seeing opportunities everywhere.[9]

My friend Denny Noland is a plumber. Denny found Christ in a Billy Graham Crusade in 1978. He gave his trade to God. In that setting, God has used him to witness. Here is his report:

> I think the sudden difference in my life scared the men I worked with. I stopped cursing. I didn't get mad easily. I stopped hitting the bars after work. . . .
>
> I didn't force my testimony on anyone at work, but a lot of people asked why I had changed so much, and I told them what had happened. . . .
>
> The people in my shop know that I'm a Christian. One time, when I'd just returned from a Work and Witness trip to

Africa, we were having our monthly foremen's meeting. Our guest speaker was late, so the president of the company asked if I would like to tell about my trip to Africa.

I said, "Sure." I talked about Africa, and I told them what the Lord was doing in my life. I talked about how much my relationship with Jesus Christ means to me, and why I take time off from work and pay my own way to Africa to work there. As I finished speaking, the door opened and the speaker walked in.[10]

But beyond taking advantage of opportunities, we shall have to take initiative to do some things on purpose. In the spring and fall, as part of my teaching at Nazarene Seminary in Kansas City and as part of my minister of outreach responsibilities at First Church of the Nazarene, Kansas City, I set aside each Thursday night to go calling. I always try to take students and laypeople with me. The goal of our calling is to witness to people about Jesus, share the gospel, and invite folks to accept the Lord—when the Holy Spirit opens the door. In the summer I do not carry on such a specific calling program. Would you believe that we see far more people won to Christ in the spring and fall than in the summer? Intentional witness and personal evangelism is blessed by God.

If your skills in witnessing and personal evangelism need strengthening, two very important steps are to take a training class in personal evangelism and to go out on evangelism calls with someone who has had the privilege of seeing people accept Christ.[11] This going on calls with another is called on-the-job training. It was a major teaching practice of both Jesus and the apostle Paul.

Robert Coleman says of Jesus' on-the-job training of His disciples,

> They observed how He drew people to himself; how He won their confidence and inspired their faith; how He opened to them the way of salvation and called them to a decision.[12]

Experience shows that classroom teaching does not have a very major effect unless it is tied to on-the-job experience.

On an August 30, Nazarene Theological Seminary and 18 area churches launched into the fall with a personal evangelism banquet. Seventeen people gave testimony, and they were primarily testimonies of how they had found Jesus in recent months. One was Mark Lockard, owner of Crescent Cleaners in Belton and Harrisonville, Mo. He tells how personal soul winner Tom Decker impacted his life:

> I attended church for 32 years because it was the right thing to do. Good people go to church. Unfortunately, the gospel was never really shared with me. I believed that I wasn't worthy of the Lord's love and that I could never be good enough to get into heaven. On October 22 of last year, however, Tom Decker shared the gospel with me and told me that I am somebody because God loves me. By the grace of Jesus Christ, I was saved.
>
> My whole life was changed. I have a confidence and assurance that has changed my relationships. I have a peace that I've never had before. I'm so grateful for that.[13]

The Tom Decker who led Mark Lockard to the Lord was won to Christ about five years previously when, after he visited our church, I took two young men from our church to call on him. Over barbecued beef we shared the gospel with Tom. A few days later he prayed to receive Christ. One of the persons on the call was Joe Benson, a seminary student. Later Joe told me he would have never gone out on an evangelism call except that I required him to do it. I asked him when he would have developed his skills in personal evangelism. He said he didn't know—maybe after he had pastored a few years.

You see, Joe was being real honest with me. He was admitting his fear. But on-the-job experience helped break the fear barrier for him.

Pray for the Right Questions

Years ago, Paul Orjala, missionary and professor, taught what he called the best method of evangelism. Of his prospects, he says, "I pray God will cause them to ask me the right questions." They can't get angry when you answer their questions, can they?

Earlier I led you through the steps I'd traveled to come out of my fear. Let me add some detail. Dr. Kennedy has taught us to ask diagnostic questions under the right conditions. For instance, "Tom, have you come to the place in your life where you know for certain if you died tonight you'd go to heaven?" I had been on three calls at Dr. Kennedy's school. I had not led anyone to Christ using that approach. I returned to Kansas City and told my students I'd call on their prospects. A student approached me and asked me to call with him on Jerry and his family. Jerry's family had recently been attending the little church the student pastored. We drove 70 miles to Jerry's community. We were warmly greeted by Jerry, his wife, and child.

I was nervous. It was my first time since returning home to try to present the gospel. Besides that, Jerry's relatives kept arriving at the front door. Jerry decided since I was coming to visit, he should invite all his relatives over. Soon there were 11 adults and 5 children milling about the house. I was praying. Remember Paul Orjala's advice: "Pray that God will cause them to ask you the right question." Just then Jerry asked me a question: "Rev. Shaver, you're a minister. Maybe you can tell me. Our little boy died in infancy. *If my wife or I are privileged enough to get to heaven,* will we recognize our little boy as our little boy?" (Italics mine.)

I said, "Jerry, we do believe we will recognize our loved ones in heaven. The issue is if you and your wife get to heaven. May I tell you how a person may know for sure he or she is going to heaven?" He responded, "Oh, please do."

In a few minutes, Jerry's wife called us all to the kitchen for a huge fried shrimp dinner—11 adults, 5 children, the student pastor, and me. At an appropriate time in the table conversation, I told them all of Jerry's question. I asked if they would like to hear what I promised to tell Jerry. They did! That night I shared the gospel with that roomful of people. That night 9 adults prayed to receive Christ as Savior. Seven said they weren't sure they'd had an answer yet but would keep searching. The other 2 gave clear testimony to their salvation. The next week the student told me they had a record attendance at their little church on Sunday because Jerry brought his family.

I learned that when we are committed to witness and win souls, the Holy Spirit goes before us. He prepares people. He works. Witnessing was God's idea before it was ever mine or yours. God yearns for these people to be saved even more than we do.

Earlier Bill Bright taught us to leave the results of our witness up to God. Yet let me emphasize that everyone used in personal evangelism expects to find interested people led across his or her pathway. There is a burden not only to give the witness but to see the person won to Jesus. There is great confidence in the drawing of the Holy Spirit.

Faith Expanded to Meet Witness Specifications

"If you want to know the worth of a human soul, try to save one," said Phillips Brooks.[14] The task is no easy one. For most of us, to see one soul won to Christ will take great faith.

Most of us who are Christians not only have trusted Christ for our salvation but also have developed other areas of faith. For example, in my early Christian life, I learned to trust God for finances. When another new area of challenge for finances arose, I could apply my past faith experiences to the new need—because they were so much alike. I call it case-for-case transfer of faith. Small financial need—I trusted God. Medium financial need—with a little stretch of my soul, I could trust God again. But when I moved to a new area like healing or soul winning, the stretch of the soul was more demanding.

Gordon MacDonald speaks of being pushed into a new sphere of reality, into an unexpected challenge only to discover "my faith was not enlarged enough." Remember when Jesus was sleeping in the boat and a furious squall came upon the boat and disciples (Mark 4:35-41). The disciples are paralyzed with fear, but Jesus stills the storm. Jesus questions, "Do you still have no faith?"

MacDonald responds:

> Didn't they have at least a little bit of faith when they chose to follow Him in the first place? Of course. But He was speaking of that dynamic element of faith, the part that is supposed to enlarge to fit each circumstance. And their faith had clearly not yet expanded to meet storm specifications.[15]

"Faith . . . expanded to meet storm specifications." And we need something just like that—faith expanded to meet witnessing and soul-winning specifications! Our faith expands when we read or hear of it in others. When I read *Rees Howells, Intercessor,*[16] my faith expanded to trust God for finance. When I read Ann Kiemel Anderson's chapter, "The Art of Being Human," in *The Art of Sharing Your Faith,*[17] my faith leaped to believe God can use me to win others to Christ. Even as you read this chapter, God is challenging you to believe Him for souls—in some cases, even specific persons—to be won to Christ!

Have you ever been able to picture yourself as a witness

and soul winner? Gordon Cosby counsels us, "Let Jesus Christ
. . . resuscitate within us all those wild hopes that world has
taught us to distrust."[18] Pray your dreams and dream your
prayers. And dream big, my brother, my sister! Pray big!

* * *

Your Response

As you have read this chapter, you have had some
thoughts about what you would need to do to overcome fear.
It has been suggested that most of us work through our fears
by progressive steps. What is the next step you need to take
this week to move forward in overcoming fear? Is it

_____ a. Inviting a fringe family of your church into a social
activity?

_____ b. Inviting a loved one or friend or neighbor into a social
activity?

_____ c. Witnessing to a person on your prospect list?

_____ d. Committing yourself to a personal evangelism training
class?

_____ e. Arranging to go on a personal evangelism call where
you can observe the gospel being shared?

_____ f. Other _____

Now complete this statement.

In order to move forward in overcoming my fear of witnessing and with God's help, this next week I will _____

_____

_____

_____

Report the result to a trusted friend next week. Or report to
the class studying this book.

5

What Will You Tell Them?

A few weeks before I wrote this chapter, I received a long-distance phone call from a pastor. He was concerned and sincere. He had two degrees from a Nazarene college. He had pastored several years, yet he had a question. He had phoned four different denominational or institutional offices before he phoned me. He still needed an answer. Here was his question: "How do you make a pastoral call?"

I was proud of the pastor for seeking out the answer. I felt sad that he didn't know how to make such calls. As I've thought about this more, I'm convinced he was being very honest about an issue that bothers many of us. We have discovered a wonderful truth, we have experienced a great spiritual reality, but our delivery system for getting it to others hasn't been adequately prepared. If a pastor could have such a problem, it is no surprise that many laypeople could too.

I Don't Know What to Say

Over the years, I have heard many Christians lament their lack of witness. Commonly, I hear a statement like this: "I know I should witness, Pastor, but I don't know what to say."

When Jesus commissioned His disciples to witness in Luke 24:46-49, the message included seemed simple. Christ told them:

> This is what is written: The Christ will suffer and rise from the dead on the third day, and repentance and forgiveness of sins will be preached in his name to all nations, beginning at Jerusalem. You are witnesses of these things. I am going to send you what my Father has promised; but stay in the city until you have been clothed with power from on high.

The central truth in this passage is that Christ suffered and rose from the dead. His resurrection on the third day fulfills prophecy (Matt. 16:21), thus indicating God's control of the situation. This is an actual historic event. The fact of Christ's resurrection from the dead means He is alive today and at work in the world. In the light of Christ's actions, how are people to respond? They are to repent, or turn from sin. The preaching of this message in Christ's name implies that faith is to be put in Him. The benefit that comes from this repentance and faith is the forgiveness of sins. I know of no place in Scripture that gives a simple five-point outline of presenting the gospel. But certainly the Luke passage shows us that all people need to hear of Christ's death and resurrection, repentance, faith, and the forgiveness of sins.

One of the best examples of evangelistic preaching in the Bible is Peter's sermon preached after the outpouring of the Spirit and recorded in Acts 2:14-41. Leighton Ford sees four distinctive marks in the sermon:

1. It appealed to Scripture as authoritative.

2. It centered on Jesus Christ.

3. It brought conviction and concern to the hearers.

4. It called for immediate and definite response.[1]

Peter's sermon also points out that the listeners' sin played a part in crucifying Christ. "God has made this Jesus, whom you crucified, both Lord and Christ" (v. 36). The appeal is for the purpose of demonstrating that God has fulfilled His promises in Jesus. What are people to do? They are to repent and be baptized in the name of Christ. The baptism indicates both faith and public profession. Once again the benefit is the forgiveness of sins. There is also the promise of the gift of the Spirit. The basics are stressed—the death and resurrection of Christ, repentance, faith, and the forgiveness of sins, as Jesus said in Luke 24.

We have seen that Paul's synagogue preaching and his preaching at the Areopagus were different. The difference was because of the background of the hearers. The spiritual decision process model helped us understand our need to give the elements of the message based on the prospect's readiness. The question we are to ask ourselves to help gauge our witness is, "How much do they know?" Paul's Areopagus message grabs people's attention where they are, gives far less detail about Christ, and emphasizes judgment and repentance. It may have been a first effort by Paul, which would be followed by more specific preaching later. A given witness should be based on the prospect's readiness and openness in that moment. As the prospect becomes more hungry, more message can be given. Eventually Christ's death and resurrection, repentance, faith, and the forgiveness of sins can be stressed. The goal is to see the prospect has enough facts so that he or she will repent and choose to follow Christ.

In the days of Jesus and Paul, the average person lived in fear of demons, fate, or magic. So when Jesus repeatedly defeated the demons, and Paul cast the demon out of the slave girl in Philippi (Acts 16:16-18), onlookers were attracted. Paul praises Christ in Col. 2:15, "Having disarmed the powers and authorities, he made a public spectacle of them, triumphing over them by the cross." This Christ was the answer to their everyday fears. Michael Green says, "Perhaps the greatest single factor which appealed to the man in the street was deliverance, deliverance from demons, from Fate, from magic."[2]

When we remember that people of that day responded to the gospel because it met a felt need, then our witness for today is informed. What are the most felt needs of the society in which I live? In the United States of America, I believe two of the greatest felt needs are to have self-worth and to have power to live daily. Remember Dan Durick's testimony as a restaurant executive: he had searched for self-worth in his business endeavors, but Christ gave him a greater sense of value. The Jews to whom Jesus preached and the synagogues where Paul preached included people with a high view of the law and a deep sense of failure and sin. Forgiveness was important to them. The need for forgiveness is still a real need today, but it is often submerged below other issues. Many people I know are so overwhelmed by the difficulties of life that power for living may be Christianity's attraction for them. In this case, my witness may emphasize regeneration more than justification. I might say, "Bill, before I met Christ, I lived with a constant sense of worry because the problems of life were so overwhelming. Now with Christ in my life, there is a power resource for problem solving. There is a freshness and challenge to life. When God's power brings the answer, there is peace." Think of the people you know in your country and circle of friends. Their felt need should help shape your testimony.

But even after we have recognized the need of shaping our testimony to have special appeal to our prospects, we are helped if we can have some basic guidelines or structure for our witness. Shortly I will speak to this issue. But before I do . . .

Different Spiritual Needs

Though it is true that people have different *felt needs,* we as Christians realize there are different levels of actual spiritual need. We may enter the discussion at the place of felt need. We should finish the witness—or the witnesses, because several messages may be needed when the prospect is not fully open—at the point of real need.

We will need to cross the barriers of culture, race, language, and class to be sure the gospel is planted among all types of people. Earlier we emphasized witnessing to those with whom we are comfortable. While that is generally true, there will be times God will have a special adventure for you. By divine providence, He will take you beyond your comfort zone. You will recall that in Luke 24:46-49, Jesus commissions the disciples to go "to all nations." In Acts 1:8, Christ promised power for witnessing—not only to Judea and Samaria, but "to the ends of the earth." Christ seems to have special concern that our circle of influence continues to widen. Christian witnesses should have a sensitive heart and discerning eye to make that happen. While a few Christians have received a missionary gift that makes them especially effective in a cross-cultural ministry, most of us will have more limited opportunities in life to help reach another group. I've experienced a great joy in helping to start a Cambodian ministry here in my city. Who do you know in a different group of people who needs Jesus now?

Within our immediate circle of acquaintances there will be those whose spiritual life is obviously lacking. Jesus spoke of leaving 99 sheep to seek 1 who had strayed away (Luke 15:4). These are people who have known Christ but have drifted or fallen away from Him and who give no indication of spiritual life today. They are backslidden.[3] They need to return to Jesus. Care must be exercised in approaching many of these people. Often they have negative or bitter feelings about God or the church. We probably will find it necessary to develop a loving friendship with them before we can expect that they will listen to the gospel afresh. We must earn the right to be heard.

Once sufficient friendship has developed so that the backslider trusts us, we may talk to him or her about the gospel. Sometimes after deep trust has been nurtured, we may ask, "Janice, how are things going for you in your relationship with Christ?" This gives the backslider the opportunity to open up his or her need. Sometimes the backslider will admit to not living for God but will claim salvation based on a past acceptance of Christ. In this case it is best to deal with the person in the language he or she understands. Ask one or all of these questions:

1. Are you now in fellowship with Jesus Christ?

2. What has Jesus Christ done in your life this week that indicates your relationship with Him is what it ought to be?

3. Is your relationship with Christ as meaningful and satisfying as you wish it to be?[4]

If this prospect is responding to these questions with a sense of need, my decision question would be, "Janice, would you like to renew your relationship with Christ?" Notice that this line of discussion does not debate the loss of the person's salvation; rather it emphasizes the renewing of relationship. I understand the Scripture to teach that Christ's blessings (including eternal life) only come to us as we are "in Christ" (Ephesians 1). I am reminded (and would remind my friend) that Christ is saying, "Here I am! I stand at the door and knock. If anyone hears my voice and opens the door, I will come in and eat with him, and he with me" (Rev. 3:20). Further, I would share that the people to whom Christ gives this challenge are described in verse 16: "So, because you are lukewarm—neither hot nor cold—I am about to spit you out of my mouth."

The concern of God is to take people beyond conversion. Note the purpose of preaching in Col. 1:28: "We proclaim him, admonishing and teaching everyone with all wisdom, so that we may present everyone perfect in Christ." When the news reached headquarters in Jerusalem that Samaria had received the Word of God under Philip, a high-powered preaching team was dispatched for a second round of revival preaching. Peter and John prayed for these Samaritan believers "that they might receive the Holy Spirit" (Acts 8:15). For the exemplary Christians at Thessalonica (1 Thess. 1:3-7), Paul expressed concern that something was lacking in their faith (3:10). Paul then prayed that God himself would "sanctify you through and through" (5:23). Even more, Paul was certain He would do it (v. 24).

There is an emerging hunger in the Christian world today for a life of victory over sin and power for living and witness. The hunger is expressed in books like Charles Colson's *Loving God.*[5] Often the Christian world senses the hunger but doesn't know the answer. Thank God, there is an answer! We need to experience it and share it. Christians need to witness to other Christians about the possibility of the sanctified life. I urge Christians to ask this question of other Christians, "Since you have found Christ, have you also made the wonderful discovery of what it is to be sanctified entirely?" Sometimes I alter the question so that my final words are "what it is to be filled with the Spirit." The change is dependent on my knowledge of the person's background and understanding. Then I will use my adaptation of Campus Crusade's circles representing spiritual life. I find that a simple explanation of these circles turns on many lights for people.

Following are three circles representing the possible lives people live. The key explains what each symbol stands for. The scripture gives the Bible description of each life.

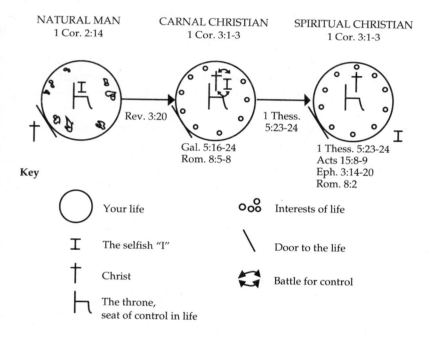

NATURAL MAN
1 Cor. 2:14

CARNAL CHRISTIAN
1 Cor. 3:1-3

SPIRITUAL CHRISTIAN
1 Cor. 3:1-3

Rev. 3:20

1 Thess.
5:23-24

Gal. 5:16-24
Rom. 8:5-8

1 Thess. 5:23-24
Acts 15:8-9
Eph. 3:14-20
Rom. 8:2

Key

Your life

Interests of life

The selfish "I"

Door to the life

Christ

Battle for control

The throne,
seat of control in life

Then I may ask, "Which circle most represents your present life?"[6] Further: "Which circle most represents the life you'd like to have?" Often with an explanation of the conditions of consecration, cleansing, and faith, people are ready to pray.[7]

When you share your testimony or witness to people—whether you witness to salvation or entire sanctification—you are an expert. You are telling what Jesus did for you. There is no argument against it. It is Peter's "We cannot help speaking about what we have seen and heard" (Acts 4:20). It is John's "The life appeared; we have seen it and testify to it, and we proclaim to you the eternal life, which was with the Father and has appeared to us" (1 John 1:2). Take courage! You are the authority on what happened to you.

Rapport

All of us feel uncomfortable with approaching a person and immediately asking, "Are you saved?" It's too abrupt. It's too personal. It doesn't fit the normal patterns of conversation.

Questions about one's spiritual welfare are personal too. We must earn the right to be heard, to ask personal questions. The process to earning that right is called establishing rapport. Let me define rapport: a deep enough understanding of each other so as not to be afraid to share with each other deep, personal things.

Jesus builds rapport with the woman at the well by making a request, "Will you give me a drink?" (John 4:7). When Jesus meets Zacchaeus, who had taken initiative by climbing a tree to be sure he could see Him, Jesus' words were not immediately religious. Rather, they would build confidence for a future conversation: "Zacchaeus, come down immediately. I must stay at your house today" (Luke 19:5). To the disciples of John, Jesus begins with a very open-ended question, "What do you want?" (John 1:38). They may say as much or as little as they desire.

Even in the bold preaching of Peter in Acts, another event becomes the natural bridge into his message. The Pentecost sermon (2:14-41) is built on the amazement of those who have just seen the results of the outpouring of the Spirit.

His message in 3:12-26 is built on the astonishment of the crowd in observing the healed lame man.

When we wish to witness to a person, we too need to build on previous conversations. A good starting place is to discover what's important to people in their everyday secular life, even as Jesus talked about a drink with the thirsty woman at the well. The letters H-E-L-P suggest four areas of life most people are comfortable to discuss. H stands for home, E for employment or job, L for loved one, and P for pleasures or pastimes (hobbies, sports, etc.). As people relax in discussing these issues, move to a more significant topic. Ask about their church background. Church background is less threatening than talking about one's spiritual life. You might tie into what they've told you about their childhood. For example, say, "Tom and Frances, did you have the privilege of attending Sunday School or church as a child?" You have now moved from secular life to church background. If they have visited your church, it will be natural to discuss your church a bit. Then you are at the place where you are ready to share your testimony. This natural progression of subjects is not threatening. Following this paragraph, I include an outline of a way to present the gospel.[8] Look only at Item "I. The Introduction." Sense the natural flow as we move from their secular life to their church background to our church to testimony. (I realize this outline looks complicated at this stage. Hold steady. At this point, I only ask you to look at the first four items under "I. The Introduction.")

Outline of the Gospel Presentation

I. THE INTRODUCTION
   A. Their secular life
   B. Their church background

C. Our church

D. Testimony—personal and/or church

E. Two Diagnostic Questions:
1. *Remember the children's prayer, "If I should die before I wake . . ."?* Have you come to the place in your life where you know for certain that if you were to die today you would go to heaven?
Transitional question: Would you like for me to share with you how I made that discovery and how you can know it too?
2. Suppose that you were to die tonight and stand before God and He were to say to you, "Why should I let you into My heaven?" What would you say?

II. THE GOSPEL

A. Grace
1. Eternal life *including heaven* is a free gift (Rom. 6:23).
2. It is not earned or deserved (Eph. 2:8-9).
Illustration: Parent giving gift to child.

B. *Humanity*
1. *Each person has sinned* (Rom. 3:23).
2. *A person can't save himself or herself* (Eph. 2:9).
Illustration: One rotten egg in omelet.

C. God
1. Is merciful; He wants you to go to heaven (2 Pet. 3:9).
2. Is just; therefore holds us accountable for our sins (Rom. 6:23).
Illustration: Young lawyer—savior, judge, *or criminals before God.*

D. Christ
   1. Who He is—the God-man (John 1:1, 14).
   2. What He did—
      a. He suffered and died for our sins (Isa. 53:6).
      b. He arose from the dead and is in heaven pre-
      paring a place for us (John 14:1-2).
      c. Offers us a gift of eternal life (1 John 5:11-12).
      Illustration: Transfer of iniquity, using a book.
E. Faith
   1. What it is not—Mere intellectual assent or temporal
   faith (James 2:19).
   2. What it is—Repenting of our sins and trusting
   Christ alone for eternal life (Mark 1:15 *and John
   1:12*).
   Illustration: Transfer weight to another chair.

III. THE COMMITMENT
   A. The clarifying question: Does this make sense to you?
   B. The commitment question: Would you like to receive
   Christ and the gift of eternal life (Rev. 3:20)?
   C. The clarification of commitment. *(Rev. 3:20 and 19)*
   Illustration: penny jar.
   D. The prayer of commitment.
   E. The assurance of eternal life (John 6:47).

IV. BEGINNING NURTURE
   A. Witness
   B. Worship
   C. Bible Study
   D. Prayer
   E. Perseverance

A Planned Approach

Paul has told us that the gospel "is the power of God for the salvation of everyone who believes" (Rom. 1:16). Many believe that learning a plan of salvation or a planned approach of sharing the gospel is very effective. Such a position does not mean a particular plan saves a person. It is simply a vehicle for delivering the Good News. Only the gospel is the power of God for salvation.

Most of us believe a pastor will preach better if he or she prays and prepares the message before standing to preach it. Most of us believe a Christian is benefited by memorizing scriptures that may be shared with others under the right circumstances. Most of us do better in presenting any truth— secular or spiritual—if we have thought through the needs or questions of our hearers in advance. You will give a more effective witness if you think through your presentation rather than begin spontaneously. Get the basics into your mind and heart in advance.

Earlier I said that the Bible does not give a simple five-point outline to be used for sharing the gospel. However, we have noted certain basic truths that show up numbers of times in both the instructions of Jesus about witnessing and early preaching. These include Christ's death and resurrection, repentance, faith, and the forgiveness of sins. There are also basic creeds or forms of confession of faith in the New Testament: Rom. 10:9; 1 Cor. 12:3; 1 Pet. 1:18-22.[9] William Abraham says the church found it essential to do several things to guard its intellectual treasures. One was to develop basic summaries of the faith, which became ways to identify the Christian community.[10] If such is true, why would it not be appropriate to assemble basic scriptures and principles explaining how a person may come into right relationship with God? Let me reiterate that the gospel outline on pages 95-97 is such a tool.[11]

I could make a strong case for the value of a planned approach in sharing the gospel. Instead, I'll tell you this story. Fifteen days prior to my writing this page, Bill and Dot Swanson approached me after prayer meeting service in my home church. They are from the southwestern United States and are members of Long Beach, Calif., First Church of the Nazarene. They reminded me I had held a personal evangelism clinic at their church about 10 years ago when they were only month-old Christians. They listened to my lectures on evangelism, learned a gospel outline, and were assigned by their pastor to go with me on a call. When we arrived at the prospect's door, I thought she looked sick, so I asked if we should come back later. "No. Come in," she said. During a Spirit-led time in that home, the husband accepted Christ. The wife was already a Christian. The Swansons and I rejoiced as they drove me back to my room.

They couldn't wait to get rid of me. They were burdened to call on their longtime friend Ben Irwin. Since their conversion a month before, the Swansons had been trying to witness to Ben. Ben felt he had too many sins. They seemed to get no further. He had suffered a heart attack and lapsed into a coma a few days later. But this very day the doctor had called to say Ben was conscious. The Swansons witnessed to Ben again. He prayed to receive Christ, and a wonderful peace seemed to invade him. In a short time he went to be with the Lord. But this statement from the Swansons was in bright neon for me: "We had no idea what to say in witness. Now with the seminar and the call, we knew what to say." There is some hard work in learning to be a good witness for Jesus, but if we care enough about people like Ben Irwin, it's worth it.

A Good Testimony

"There is no denying the zeal and the sense of discovery that marked the witness of the early church both in their public and private testimony, both in their written and their spoken work," states Michael Green.[12] Personal witness is such a major way to spread the gospel in the Early Church that Luke reports Paul's full testimony in nearly the same detail three different times in Acts (chaps. 9; 22; 26). In other places a more limited witness is given.

Charles Swindoll says,

> On six separate occasions between Paul's third missionary journey and his trip to Rome, he stood before different audiences and presented Christ to them (Acts 22-26). Six times he stood alone. Six times he addressed unbelievers. Do you know *the method Paul used each time? His personal testimony.*[13]

Here is Paul's testimony before King Agrippa:

¹Then Agrippa said to Paul, "You have permission to speak for yourself."

So Paul motioned with his hand and began his defense: ²King Agrippa, I consider myself fortunate to stand before you today as I make my defense against all the accusations of the Jews, ³and especially so because you are well acquainted with all the Jewish customs and controversies. Therefore, I beg you to listen to me patiently.

⁴"The Jews all know the way I have lived ever since I was a child, from the beginning of my life in my own country, and also in Jerusalem. ⁵They have known me for a long time and can testify, if they are willing, that according to the strictest sect of our religion, I lived as a Pharisee. ⁶And now it is because of my hope in what God has promised our fathers that I am on trial today. ⁷This is the promise our twelve tribes are hoping to see fulfilled as they earnestly serve God day and night. O king, it is because of this hope that the Jews are accusing me. ⁸Why

should any of you consider it incredible that God raises the dead?

⁹I too was convinced that I ought to do all that was possible to oppose the name of Jesus of Nazareth. ¹⁰And that is just what I did in Jerusalem. On the authority of the chief priests I put many of the saints in prison, and when they were put to death, I cast my vote against them. ¹¹Many a time I went from one synagogue to another to have them punished, and I tried to force them to blaspheme. In my obsession against them, I even went to foreign cities to persecute them.

¹²"On one of these journeys I was going to Damascus with the authority and commission of the chief priests. ¹³About noon, O king, as I was on the road, I saw a light from heaven, brighter than the sun, blazing around me and my companions. ¹⁴We all fell to the ground, and I heard a voice saying to me in Aramaic, 'Saul, Saul, why do you persecute me? It is hard for you to kick against the goads.'

¹⁵"Then I asked, 'Who are you, Lord?'

"'I am Jesus, whom you are persecuting,' the Lord replied. ¹⁶'Now get up and stand on your feet. I have appeared to you to appoint you as a servant and as a witness of what you have seen of me and what I will show you. ¹⁷I will rescue you from your own people and from the Gentiles. I am sending you to them ¹⁸to open their eyes and turn them from darkness to light, and from the power of Satan to God, so that they may receive forgiveness of sins and a place among those who are sanctified by faith in me.'

¹⁹"So then, King Agrippa, I was not disobedient to the vision from heaven. ²⁰First to those in Damascus, then to those in Jerusalem and in all Judea, and to the Gentiles also, I preached that they should repent and turn to God and prove their repentance by their deeds. ²¹That is why the Jews seized me in the temple courts and tried to kill me. ²²But I have had God's help to this very day, and so I stand here and testify to small and great alike. I am saying nothing beyond what the prophets and

Moses said would happen— [23]that the Christ would suffer and, as the first to rise from the dead, would proclaim light to his own people and to the Gentiles."

[24]At this point Festus interrupted Paul's defense. "You are out of your mind, Paul!" he shouted. "Your great learning is driving you insane."

[25]"I am not insane, most excellent Festus," Paul replied. "What I am saying is true and reasonable. [26]The king is familiar with these things, and I can speak freely to him. I am convinced that none of this has escaped his notice, because it was not done in a corner. [27]King Agrippa, do you believe the prophets? I know you do."

[28]Then Agrippa said to Paul, "Do you think that in such a short time you can persuade me to be a Christian?"

[29]Paul replied, "Short time or long—I pray God that not only you but all who are listening to me today may become what I am, except for these chains."

[30]The king rose, and with him the governor and Bernice and those sitting with them. [31]They left the room, and while talking with one another, they said, "This man is not doing anything that deserves death or imprisonment."

[32]Agrippa said to Festus, "This man could have been set free if he had not appealed to Caesar" *(Acts 26:1-32).*

Notice that Paul tells: (1) what life was like *before* he met Christ (vv. 4-11), (2) *how* he met Christ (vv. 12-18), and (3) what Christ has meant in his life *since* (vv. 19-23). He makes sure his testimony is filled with basic facts of the gospel such as Christ's death and resurrection. Since the testimony is his only vehicle for proclaiming the gospel in this situation, he follows it with persuasion, trying to convince Agrippa to accept Christ (vv. 27-29).

The skeptics may disbelieve Paul's doctrine or yours. They may criticize the church. The sermon may bore them. But Paul's human interest story or yours—how you found peace and purpose—that is a hard thing to put aside. It seems Agrippa was close to being persuaded. But not quite. Yet the Bible is so honest that it includes this story of one not converted. It is to keep us from being discouraged. Some of Paul's prospects didn't get saved under his witness; we should understand if some of ours don't.

I urge you to think through your testimony so that you may be more effective in presenting it. Here are some basic guidelines:

1. Make it interesting. Avoid misunderstood words like "saved" and "born again." Use picturesque language.
2. Be specific as to the time you received Christ.
3. Be practical and honest. Don't promise more than the Bible does.
4. Be warm and genuine. A smile breaks down barriers. Don't present the news of great joy with a deadpan face.
5. Describe the positive things God has done for you. One testified that when he became a Christian, he lost his job and all his friends. Few would want to find Christ if that is the result. Emphasize joy, peace, purpose, God's presence, love, sense of value.
6. Be logical. Give the before, how, and since as Paul did in his testimony. However, there is an exception. If your testimony is to lead into an extended presentation of the gospel as in the outline on pages 95-97, do *not* stress the how. If your prospect is open and the Spirit is working, you hope to ask your prospect two diagnostic questions. One is about the basis of getting into heaven. In your testimony, you do not describe the how, because your prospect will tend to parrot back to you what you said instead of giving his honest response. So if your goal is extended presentation of the gospel, don't give answers to questions you'll ask later.
7. Identify with your prospect. As you talk to your prospects, listen to what is told you about their secular and church

backgrounds. Then when you witness about your life before Christ, select truthful statements that will enable them to see themselves in your life. When I talked to a drug addict, I told of how certain sins controlled me before I found Christ. When I talked to Ruth with her good church background, I stressed my regular church attendance but no certainty of eternal life before I met Christ.

8. If your witness is leading into a gospel presentation similar to the outline I've presented on pages 95-97, be sure you include at least one sentence about receiving the certainty of eternal life. Your main thrust should be the benefits of the gospel here and now, but at least one allusion to eternal life is needed to make your first diagnostic question logical.[14]

How does your testimony or witness come across to an unsaved person? Earlier you read Dan Durick's testimony, which was given in church. Following is the testimony of Elsa Harkin of the Kansas City Blue Hills Church. This is a testimony as Elsa would give in a home setting. After telling her early days of being raised in church, she brings us to the place of her marriage:

There were many problems that arose during my marriage. The use of alcohol entered in as a means to sort of push aside the problems of the day. On weekends I'd go where the parties were, and this would provide an escape from the problems at home. But all in all I became a very depressed person with no energy to carry out daily tasks and chores. I'd go to work and was able to hold my job, but the thought of going home afterward would just seem to weigh me down. There was a feeling of worthlessness to myself and to my family. My life had no direction, no goals; it seemed as if my future was hopelessly anchored in the . . . now. I knew there had to be more to life than this.

One day I began to read my Bible . . . Those times I did read the Bible gave me . . . a lift. It was like I'd been energized.

104

This experience jogged my memory enough to bring back some of the things I'd heard during my church attendance . . .

One evening a member from Blue Hills Church came by, looking for my daughter, who had been attending their services. She wasn't home, so he began to talk with me. Incidentally, I failed to mention that once just prior to this meeting, I had prayed that the Lord would help me find a church I could attend and be faithful in doing so. [The man] . . . began to ask me questions that really made me stop and think about my life, and just where I stood right then. He offered to share the gospel with me, and I was able to receive the gift of eternal life that evening.

Since I made that decision, my life has not been the same. Not only did I receive eternal life, but also trials, problems, and situations that seemed to plague me so much before didn't seem so hard to deal with. Those depressed episodes I had have been changed to purposeful work activities, whether it's cleaning my house, shopping, working, or studying—they can all be seen from a different point of view. It's almost as if I received a new lease on life, one that won't expire. There is hope where there used to be none. Those deep feelings of worthlessness are gone, and I'm interested in reaching out to others and letting them know what God can do for them.

One of the things that really impressed me was seeing two snapshots of myself before and after I made my decision. There was a difference in my life I could definitely feel, but those pictures really showed the difference in my facial expressions. Christ has really made a change in my life. . . .

The Gospel and God's Presence

Michael Green says,

All Christians were convinced that Jesus Christ was God's last word to man, the one who brought as much of God to us as we could appreciate in the only terms we could take it in, the terms of a human life; the one who is dying and rising again was manifestly vindicated in his claims and achievement. This they all believed in common: their modes of expressing it depended to a large extent on their own intellectual and spiritual background and on that of their hearers.[15]

We will present Jesus Christ, God's great last Word! As we move beyond witness to sharing the facts of the gospel, certain basic truths need to be heard and understood. I suggest these basic truths are well covered by the outline on pages 95-97. They are grace, humanity (including sin), God, Christ, and faith (including repentance). The scope of this book does not permit a full discussion of how to do that. You may be exposed to that in more detail by listening to the audiotape *Personal Evangelism Call* or viewing the video *A Personal Evangelism Call on Mike and Janet*. Consider taking a step of faith by becoming involved in an extended personal evangelism class as explained in Beverly Burgess' *Personal Evangelism Training Leader's Manual.*[16]

Is God still raising up witnesses in our day? Consider Lee Atwater's testimony. He was the National Committee chairman for the United States Republican party, and one of the most politically powerful men in the country. He was called the "pit bull" of American politics because his methods were so vicious. But after diagnosis of an inoperable brain tumor, something changed Atwater. He said,

> I have found Jesus Christ. It's that simple. He's made a difference, and I'm glad I've found Him while there's still time . . . I don't hate anybody anymore. For the first time in my life, I don't hate somebody . . . I hope every one of you will find what I've found.[17]

Along with his testimony, Atwater made apology and restitution to those he had mistreated. And the national press has been unwittingly helping to get out the witness. The apostle Paul, Dan Durick, Elsa Harkin, Lee Atwater, and you and me—we can all tell them of Jesus. Everybody who knows Jesus can witness. And "somebody you know needs Jesus now."

When witnessing seems hard, remember Paul. After giving his testimony before a Jerusalem crowd, he came under accusation from the Sanhedrin and the guard of Roman soldiers. The cost of witnessing must have seemed very high! Acts 23:11 says, "The following night the Lord stood near Paul and said, 'Take courage! As you have testified about me in Jerusalem, so you must also testify in Rome.'" The same is true for you and me.

*　　*　　*

Your Response

Write out your testimony based on the guidelines given in this chapter. After you've written it and studied your testimony, put it away. Then, prayerfully, try to share your testimony in word with at least one person this week. Share the results with a trusted friend or the class if you are part of one studying the book.

6

Finally—a Decision

It will be the most frightening question some of you will ever ask: "Joe, would you like to receive Christ and His gift of eternal life?" Yet you will do it. And Joe will say, "Yes, I would." The joy you experience as you pray with Joe to accept the Savior will be so great that you will remember it more readily than your fear. Deep inside you know that for Joe and you—finally—it will be a decision.

The Influence of a Life

Mickey Cohen, infamous American gangster of the 1950s, professed he had accepted Christ. His Christian friend Bill Jones later confronted him about his lack of a changed life. Mickey responded, "So what's the matter with being a Christian gangster?"[1] We all smile. We *know* that professing to belong to Jesus and living like Jesus have to go together.

My friend Jim Bates says lots of professing Christians are supplying unbelievers with pain pills. The so-called Christian's inconsistent life is immediately noticed by unsaved friends. The Spirit of God has been convicting them about their need for Christ and His salvation. Then they remember the inconsistency of the "Christian's" walk. The unsaved reason, Look at him. He's supposed to be a Christian. I live that good. I guess I'm OK as I am. What relief from the pain of conviction! The troubled sinner has just been given a pain pill by a professing Christian. Certainly we do not want profession without demonstration.

What attracted the ordinary man to Christianity in its early days? The appeal included the lives of Christians, the warmth of their fellowship, the moral qualities of their lives, the enthusiasm they manifested, the freedom from the fear of judgment, the deliverance from evil powers, and the enjoyment of knowing Christ now.[2] I've heard it said, "A saint is someone whose life makes it easier to believe in God." When Susan prayed to receive Christ in her home after hearing the gospel, I asked her what had convinced her. She said it was the change she saw in her recently converted husband.

If words without works are hypocrisy, then we must say that works without words are inadequate. Sometimes we will do kind and loving deeds and say, "My life is my witness." This does not excuse us from verbal witness. I do not mean that every good work has to be followed immediately by verbal witness. No, there are times when the witness is appropriate only after many good works. But eventually and ultimately, the next loving gesture after good works will be to tell the Good News.

A few days ago I heard a remarkable report on the 5:30 P.M. television news. The commentator was interviewing the adult children of an elderly California couple who had been on an automobile trip and had become stranded in the mountains in deep snow. The couple and the car were not found for weeks. But before her death, the aged mother had written letters. She told how they had run out of food. When gasoline was gone, they had no heat for the car. Nothing about the letters indicated panic. As a matter of fact, the mother described with what peace the father died.

But something about the story was very incomplete until we heard two quotes from the mother's letter: "Dad went to be with the Lord today . . . His last words were, 'Thank the Lord.'"[3]

The elderly man's peaceful death only had meaning when there was verbal explanation. Everyone's question would be "What was the secret of their peace?" Only the effort by the children to get the story told gave meaning to the death for others beyond the immediate family. Our godly living must be followed by an explanation—"Jesus is the reason!"

Munoz had been arrested for drunkenness in Santiago, Chile. While being escorted to jail, two Christian men requested permission to take Munoz and care for him. The police agreed. The two Christians fed him, cared for him, found him a job, and told him about Jesus. Here was the result:

> The gospel meant a new life for Munoz. He began to repair shoes and was able to make a simple living for his family. He began to talk to his neighbors about the love of God that was changing his life. Step by step, he found himself sober, employed and industrious; soon he was leading a group of neighbors in worship.
>
> It was not easy to be their leader, for he could not read. He had to memorize the Bible verses that his wife read to him. He explained the verses to his friends in terms of their daily lives and hungers. Before long, he became the pastor of a new congregation of 70 members and had 150 children in a Sunday School. He still made his living as a shoemaker.[4]

What would have been the result for Munoz if his two friends fed him, cared for him, found him a job, but *never told him about Jesus?*

Jesus told His followers and us, "Let your light shine before men, that they may see your good deeds and praise your

Father in heaven" (Matt. 5:16). The purpose of the deeds is to bring praise to our Heavenly Father. If we do deeds of kindness but do not give witness to Christ, the recipients will give glory to us for being so good. If we proclaim Jesus, they will give glory to Christ who has changed us. Christians are the one group in society charged with the task of bringing people into a transforming relationship with God through Christ. We will need verbal witness to do it.

Will You Marry Me?

Here is Paul's description of ministry in 2 Cor. 5:11-21:

[11]Since, then, we know what it is to fear the Lord, we try to persuade men. What we are is plain to God, and I hope it is also plain to your conscience. [12]We are not trying to commend ourselves to you again, but are giving you an opportunity to take pride in us, so that you can answer those who take pride in what is seen rather than in what is in the heart. [13]If we are out of our mind, it is for the sake of God; if we are in our right mind, it is for you. [14]For Christ's love compels us, because we are convinced that one died for all, and therefore all died. [15]And he died for all, that those who live should no longer live for themselves but for him who died for them and was raised again.

[16]So from now on we regard no one from a worldly point of view. Though we once regarded Christ in this way, we do so no longer. [17]Therefore, if anyone is in Christ, he is a new creation; the old has gone, the new has come! [18]All this is from God, who reconciled us to himself through Christ and gave us the ministry of reconciliation: [19]that God was reconciling the world to himself in Christ, not counting men's sins against them. And he has committed to us the message of reconciliation. [20]We are therefore Christ's ambassadors, as though God were making his appeal through us. We implore you on Christ's behalf: Be reconciled to God. [21]God made him who had no sin

to be sin for us, so that in him we might become the righteousness of God.

In this passage Paul tells us some of the greatest truths about the meaning of Christ's death (vv. 15, 19, 21) and our response to that death (vv. 15, 17). He gives the motive for his ministry and ours—"Christ's love compels us" (v. 14). He gives Christian witness a different description—they are Christ's ambassadors. Good ambassadors faithfully deliver the message of their king or president. They do not have the right to develop their own message. Further ambassadors don't just deliver the message to the hearers and feel their job is done. They are out to get a favorable response to the message for the sake of their king. Thus ambassadors for Christ deliver Christ's message and then urge their hearers to accept it and be changed by it. Notice Paul's choice of words—"we try to persuade men" (v. 11), "as though God were making his appeal through us" (v. 20), "we implore you on Christ's behalf" (v. 20). Paul's plan includes both proclamation and persuasion. It includes both witnessing and winning. Paul's gospel plan has witness in its introduction, the facts of the gospel, and persuasion in the commitment (see pages 95-97).

The element of persuasion, so stressed by Paul, is implied in definitions of evangelism that may not use the term *persuasion*. William Abraham defines evangelism as "that set of *international* activities which is governed by the goal of *initiating people* into the kingdom of God for the first time" (italics mine).[5] Michael Green says, "The Gospel is God's summons, through the act of preaching, to the listener to make the decision which will usher him into a new dimension of existence."[6] We would add that "witness" could be substituted for the word "preaching."

Let me talk to you married gentlemen a minute. (Ladies, you can listen.) Men, remember when you courted your wife?

You were so taken by her that you sent her flowers, you took her to dinner, you brought her gifts. The love you felt could only be expressed by many kind deeds. Yet you did not expect the girl to marry you just because of your kind and loving deeds. There was more, men. You proclaimed your love. You told her, "I love you." Yet few of you were married because of the verbal expression. There was more. There was a specific call to commitment: "Will you marry me?" All of these issues are equally true in the spiritual realm. There is living a life of loving deeds (cultivation), there is the witness of words (proclamation), there is the call to commitment (persuasion). (This is a good time to look again at the Spiritual Decision Process Model on page 49.) For the prospect to respond positively to Jesus Christ, a verbal call to decision is expected. Our primary concern in this book has been witness. Yet we all sense that witness naturally belongs with soul winning and persuasion.

Your persuasion is no violation of the prospect's rights. The prospect has the freedom to accept or reject Christ even as your marriage proposal may receive a yes or no. I am especially sensitive to this, since my earliest overtures to my wife were rejected. She had the power to say no and did. But later, with further demonstration of love and persuasion, she said yes.

Some Christians have been reluctant to try to persuade their friends and loved ones to accept Christ because they assume that all persuasion is manipulation. They know manipulation is wrong. Such understanding must be wrong because Paul said, "Since, then, we know what it is to fear the Lord, we try to persuade men" (2 Cor. 5:11). Further he said, "As God's fellow workers we urge you not to receive God's grace in vain" (6:1). The good and godly Paul believed in persuasion.

113

James McGraw's distinction between manipulation and persuasion is helpful:

> Manipulation is that type of persuasion which is deceptively intended for the advantage of the persuader. It is the attempt to get someone to do something he probably would not do if he had all the facts, so only those facts the persuader believes will influence the person are given to him.
>
> Persuasion, on the other hand, can be used for a person's good and for the glory of God. To persuade a sinner to put his trust in Christ, to persuade a husband to stop cheating on his wife, or to persuade a distraught man not to take his own life are good ways to use words. But to persuade a teenager to try a shot of heroin, of course, is another matter.[7]

If I really believe the gospel message, I will sense the need to persuade. For my friends to find Christ is their greatest good. If I really care, I will urge them to do so. It is tragic to stand at the crossroads of life and discover that the signposts have fallen down. The "harassed and helpless" of Jesus' day (Matt. 9:36) and of ours need Christians to lead them in the way of life. It is the most compassionate and loving thing you can do to lead a person to Christ.

A Commitment Question

Since "the bent of the homo sapiens is to evade,"[8] this is all the more reason why Jesus and His witnesses should call for a decisive response.[9] Matthew's Gospel is written to bring readers to the place where "decision is imperative. Neutrality is impossible."[10] Even the stories of people in Matthew are geared to cause us to face this issue. The wise men sought Jesus wholeheartedly. Herod's response was hatred and fear. What will the reader's response be? When Jesus teaches about the wide and narrow gates (7:13-14), there is the implicit challenge to the reader to make a choice too. Even the trial of

Jesus puts the reader in the place of choice (27:11-26). In Peter's powerful Pentecost sermon, the hearers actually asked Peter what they should do (Acts 2:37). Then Peter spelled out a clarification of commitment (vv. 38-39) or what the hearers needed to do to be saved. The acceptance of baptism was the public witness that the hearer had accepted Christ (v. 41).

The church growth movement has added many benefits to the life of the church. Its sociological understandings help us know issues that influence people toward or away from the church and Christ. But in the final analysis church growth needs another element—how to lead that responding person into a relationship with Christ. There still needs to be a commitment question.

Friendship evangelism is tremendously important for the cause of Christ. Because it is less threatening than personal evangelism, many more Christians will be able to do it. But somewhere along the way, that unsaved person will need someone to challenge him or her to accept Jesus. And there will be some times when all of us will have to do some personal evangelism. Elgin was a dedicated Christian but not a flashy or extroverted person. He came into our personal evangelism training and in his loving way began sharing the gospel regularly. The last eight years of Elgin's life were some of the most exciting as he began to see people he talked to pray right in their homes.

My usual practice in asking for commitment is guided by the commitment section in the outline on page 97. The scope of this book does not allow for extensive discussion of this important issue, but I will make a few comments.[11] My typical commitment question is only asked after a person seems to indicate he or she has an understanding of the gospel. Then I would ask, "Joe, would you like to receive Christ and His gift of eternal life?" If he says yes, I show him Rev. 3:20 and clarify what accepting Christ means:

Joe, do you understand that accepting Christ means you are inviting Christ into your heart? To open the door of your heart, you must repent, that is, with God's help, turn from your sins. Do you know things in your life that are displeasing to God? Are you willing to turn from them?

To invite Christ into your heart means He comes in not only as Savior to forgive the past but also as Lord. It means from this moment on you are willing for Him to call the shots in your life. Are you willing for Him to do that?

If he is willing, I suggest we pray together. I give rather careful instructions about how we will pray in order to avoid embarrassment.

If I think my prospect is not ready to receive Christ and there may be a rejection, I change my commitment question. It becomes, "Joe, would you like to receive Christ and His gift of eternal life tonight, or is this something you need more time to think about?" Do not give this option too easily because even spiritually hungry people may tend to delay. If it is strongly apparent the regular call to commitment will bring rejection, the alternate choice of time to think prevents the hardening of a rejection position.

Follow-up and Nurture

Once a person has come to accept Christ, he or she should be started on a program of Bible study such as *Basic Bible Studies for New/Growing Christians.* [12] The convert should be assigned a spiritual adoptive parent who will care for him or her with a parent heart and guide the person in early Christian life. The support of Christian friends is so important that it is almost a mathematical equation: "If the pressure of the world is not equalled by the support of Christians the convert will be lost."[13] The whole first year of the new convert's life is critical for establishment. The issue of follow-up is vastly important and needs much attention. Once again it is beyond the scope of this book to deal extensively with that issue. I have written on the subject in the book *Conserve the Converts*.[14]

A Church Decides for Witness

Jesus invested most of His ministry time in 12 men. Someday He would be leaving, and these 12 would carry on His work. Jesus even prayed "for those who will believe in me through their message" (John 17:20). He taught, "A student is not above his teacher, but everyone who is fully trained will be like his teacher" (Luke 6:40). He trained a core of witnesses that would be like Him and would win others.

Paul had a passion to get the gospel out to people every chance he had, and because of that he targeted potential leaders who in turn would influence others. The result was the message spread more quickly. Paul invested heavily in Timothy. Then he spoke to Timothy about his future influence: "And the things you have heard me say in the presence of many witnesses entrust to reliable men who will also be qualified to teach others" (2 Tim. 2:2). How often we discover Paul reaching potential leaders: "He met a Jew named Aquila" (Acts 18:2), "a woman named Lydia, a dealer in purple cloth" (16:14), "Crispus, the synagogue ruler" (18:8), and "leaders of the Jews" (28:17). Paul influences Priscilla and Aquila, who disciple Apollos, who goes to Achaia to minister (18:26-27). This is multiplication in action. When Paul explains the place of the ministry gifts, he says, "It was he who gave some to be apostles, some to be prophets, some to be evangelists, and some to be pastors and teachers, to prepare God's people for works of service, so that the body of Christ may be built up"

(Eph. 4:11-12). Notice the professional ministry is to prepare or equip all God's people (the laity) for service. No wonder James Kennedy says, "It is more important to train a soul-winner than to win a soul . . . It is because winning a person to Christ is so important that training someone to win 10 or 100 or 1,000 people to Christ is so much more important."[15]

Paul had a Barnabas, a Silas, a Timothy, a Luke. Where is your Timothy? Are you showing someone else how to witness? Robert Coleman says, "Winning disciples who will win others and train them in discipleship is the basic strategy of evangelism."[16]

Imagine yourself committed to a witnessing and training ministry. Assume you would win two people to Christ and train those two to win others to Christ in a six-month period. Assume each one trained would follow the same pattern each six months, and all would continue faithfully for four years. I have put this idea in what I call the "Spiritual Multiplication Chart." Could you see yourself in it?

1 win and train	2 =	3 in 6 months
3 win and train	6 =	9 in 12 months
9 win and train	18 =	27 in 18 months
27 win and train	54 =	81 in 24 months
81 win and train	162 =	243 in 30 months
243 win and train	486 =	729 in 36 months
729 win and train	1,458 =	2,187 in 42 months
2,187 win and train	4,374 =	6,561 in 48 months

Not only do we need to personally become witnesses, but we need to strategically position ourselves to reach as many as possible. It means local churches will develop "a *research-based, Spirit-led strategy to reach people with the good news and to build them in the faith.*"[17] Here are some examples of intentional strategies to reach people for Christ I have seen work.

1. A Sunday School class organized with 5 people in 1975, geared to conduct class in language new people could understand. At the time of this writing, four other classes have been born from it. The original class is averaging 75 a Sunday, and 20 to 30 people join the church each year from the class.

2. A group of young adults decided to reach out to the young adults on the fringes of the church. Instead of spending all their social time with their best Christian friends in the church, these young adults began to invite the fringe young adults to dinner once a month. Before long, new young adults were being converted.

3. In the Antipolo church in the Philippines, a representative of the church will approach the "barangay" captain. This person is the political leader for a certain geographical area. The captain is asked for permission to start a new church in the new area. Often permission is gained to use the "barangay" hall. This means the church begins with the favor of the authorities. One such new church runs more than 100 in attendance each Sunday.

4. A church develops a preschool program with the intentional purpose of reaching families for Christ.

5. A Korean boy, whose father was a high priest in Confucianism, wanted education in a Christian school. The school intentionally set this requirement: each student must attend a Christian church and pass in a church bulletin. As a result, the Korean boy visited a Church of the Nazarene. Two years later, while attending a special prayer meeting, the boy came to know Christ as Savior. Today that boy is academic dean of Korea Nazarene Theological College, Dr. Shin Min Gyoo.

6. A church decides to sponsor a "Living Scenes of Christmas" outdoor Nativity display to bear witness to the community. The hope is that new people of the community

will be attracted to the church. In the first three nights of "Living Scenes," 2,500 people visit the church property.

7. Rev. Kim, Shi-chul has led an intentional strategy by Korean pastors and people to plant 70 new churches in Greater Seoul, Korea, within a five-year period.

8. In South America, Regional Director Louie Bustle has promoted this plan to be accomplished on a yearly basis:

   a. Each Christian win one (new person to Christ).

   b. Each pastor train one (person to become a pastor).

   c. Each church start one (new church).

South America is experiencing a new surge of growth.

To win a person to Christ never crosses the mind of some professing Christians. Others become deeply burdened for others and regularly share Christ with them. Others not only witness but also develop intentional strategies to reach others. We just looked at some of them. Have you ever prayed, "O God, what do You want me to do in this place to win people to Jesus?" What strategies is your church developing? Where is your Timothy?

My Decision to Be a Witness

This is a chapter on decision. We examined the need to extend our witness to a call for that unsaved person to make a decision for Christ. But there is another decision—it's your decision to be a witness. Will you make that decision?

There is "rejoicing in heaven over one sinner who repents" (Luke 15:7). What makes Jesus happy ought to make us happy. Forty-two times John's Gospel tells us that God *sent* Jesus.[18] And then Jesus sends us: "As the Father has sent me, I am sending you" (John 20:21). It is no aimless sending of Jesus or us. "You are witnesses," said Jesus (Luke 24:48).

This witnessing will mean a servant role—it is costly

business. Yet we are reminded of Jesus' words: "Just as the Son of Man did not come to be served, but to serve, and to give his life as a ransom for many" (Matt. 20:28). In turn the Savior tells us, "Go and make disciples of all nations" (28:19). He longs for His house to be full (Luke 14:23). We shall only do it by God's power—the power of the gospel (Rom. 1:16) and the power of the Spirit (Acts 1:8). The stakes are so high that Jesus proclaims, "What good is it for a man to gain the whole world, yet forfeit his soul?" (Mark 8:36).

Every Christian should desire to witness. Yet it should always be witness with the goal of winning. As ambassadors we implore, "Be reconciled to God" (2 Cor. 5:20). As fishers of men, we seek what all true fishermen seek—there is never full satisfaction till the fish is caught and landed. We desire to be faithful to the call of Christ—to be the men, the women that God can trust (Matt. 24:45-46). When fear attacks, I remember Paul again: "The following night the Lord stood near Paul and said, 'Take courage! As you have testified about me in Jerusalem, so you must also testify in Rome'" (Acts 23:11).

We will pray for souls and the workers to reach them (Rom. 10:1; Matt. 9:38). We will be possessed with a passion for souls—an inner consuming urge to find the lost. We will feel this way in loving gratitude for what Jesus has done for us. If we do not know the best method for reaching that unsaved person, we keep seeking for the way. If we want it badly enough, we will find the way. Ten years ago, my friend Margie Sanders was at the low point in her life. She heard the name "Jesus" on a radio broadcast. She prayed, "If You are who You say You are, then give me the peace You promised." Instantly peace came! She got on the phone and called her mother long-distance to say, "Jesus is real!" Twice more she called her mom with the same message the same night. She was burdened to witness to her family. Today 10 of her family have accepted Jesus. We may not see them come to Jesus as quickly as Margie did, or find as one prayed, "a speedy salvation." But we must remember we are in this for the long run: "At the proper time we will reap a harvest if we do not give up" (Gal. 6:9). We are part of a great stream of witnesses—over the centuries, over the years—to the present day. We shall continue the stream. There are others who need Christ.

In doing my part, I extended the stream to Roy Baker. He is a Harvard Ph.D. and a professor of accounting. Because others had prepared the way, on a September 15 evening I could go to Roy and his wife. He reports:

I'm a product of a broken home. I never really knew my mother and lived with my grandparents. Over the years, I got involved with the wrong crowds, and by the time I was 16, I had a police record as long as my arm. I ended up joining the navy. I knew about sailors' reputations and tried to live up to them. It was as if I went through a list of sins every morning to choose one for the day.

Over the years, I mellowed. I considered myself a friendly agnostic. Several things happened that could have turned my attention to the Lord. For instance, in 1954 I had cancer, but in spite of the emotional upheaval, I didn't turn to God. In 1972 I had a heart attack, and in 1973 I was divorced, but I still didn't turn to God. I decided to give up drinking alcohol and then smoking tobacco. But again, I had not accepted the Lord. Nobody had ever shared the gospel with me.

About four years ago, Arleta Andre, a member of Kansas City First Church of the Nazarene, invited my wife and me to the spring handbell concert. Everybody was so friendly that we decided to go back for a morning service and have been attending ever since.

However, being a pseudointellectual, I was hesitant to accept Christ. I talked to Pastor Shaver at church, and he offered to come over and explain Nazarene theology to me. He and two other people came to our house one evening and, after visiting awhile, Pastor Shaver asked, "Roy, if you died tonight, would you go up to heaven?" That got my attention. I really didn't know. Pastor Shaver presented the gospel to us and everything became clear—Jesus died for me.

He's done marvelous things since I received Him into my life.

Recently I've had the opportunity to counsel my students about problems, and the Lord has given me wisdom, although I'm not trained in psychology. I have a reputation around the campus now: "If you've got a problem, go to Dr. Baker. It stops at his door." As of Labor Day, I will be teaching part-time not only at the University of Missouri-Kansas City, but also at Mid-America Nazarene College. I believe this is the road to which the Lord has been leading me.[19]

When I was 5 years old, I began to be hungry to know God. For 15 years I attended Sunday School and church faithfully, but I never found Jesus. The preaching at my church was never clear on how to find Jesus. Finally when I was 20, Peter told me how he had found Jesus and how I could too. The next day I attended the Church of the Nazarene with him, and under Rev. Ralph Ferrioli's evangelistic preaching, I met Jesus. My friend Peter's testimony had given me the lead I needed. He was a witness, but neither of us knew what to call it. Since that November 20 evening, my life has been care, prayer, share.

Even with feelings of fear, I receive God's power and witness. I remember the radio speaker: "You are a witness when you are more concerned about what people think of Jesus than you are of what people think of you." There is an urgency. Amy Carmichael said, "We have all eternity to celebrate the victories but only a few hours before sunset to win them."

So the Bible has been speaking to me about my witness.

Now I need to speak to the Lord about what I will do about my witness. I determine, God helping, I will be a witness for Jesus. Remember, someone you know needs Jesus now.

Consuelo is a Filipino woman who helps our missionaries in Asia-Pacific Nazarene Theological Seminary. Consuelo had hungered to find God, and when she was younger, she used to come into her church and get on her knees and crawl from the back to the altar, hoping to find peace. At Easter time she participated in the Virgin Mary parades that would, each night of Easter week, go to a different house and pray. She never found peace; she never found joy. Then one day, somebody with soul-winning eyes invited her to a Bible study. At that Bible study she heard that Jesus could be real, and sins could be forgiven. She came to a place where she confessed her sins and accepted Jesus in September of 1979. She said, "I found peace, I found forgiveness, and I found strength to live life." She told her husband, and he accepted Jesus. In 1980 they began attending the Church of the Nazarene.

In 1981 their third child was born. Six weeks after the child was born, Consuelo woke up one morning. She heard a noise from her husband lying next to her in bed. She turned to him, and there he died suddenly. He was 30 years old. Her brother said to her, "Oh, your husband died because you changed churches." She said, "I knew that wasn't the reason. I knew my husband had gone to be with the Lord." And she said to God, "I know You have a plan for my life now; You lead me." Her neighbors watched her. Her neighbors watched the church, and they saw how the church supported her in the death of her husband. She said, "I felt more love here than I'd ever felt anyplace before in my life." She has been raising her three girls in a wonderful way, ages 20, 14, and 10. It's very expensive to send your children to high school in the Philippines. Consuelo earns 400 to 500 pesos a week, that's

$17.00 a week. Now to have no husband and to have three children to be sending to high school on $17.00 a week! "Oh," she said, "I set my tithes aside first. My mother-in-law said to me, 'You are always so happy, and you never ask us for money; how come?'" Consuelo said, "I ask God for money. He makes a way."

This is the smiling woman of the Philippines. She is so happy. She has found Jesus. She follows Him every day. Jesus is helping her raise her children. God has made her a witness. She goes out into homes. She is leading other people to Jesus. She led her mother to Jesus. She has led others to Jesus. She is guiding new Christians through *Basic Bible Studies*. All because somebody saw Consuelo with soul-winning eyes.[20] I wonder, will we see that way? Jesus said, "Look at the fields! They are ripe for harvest" (John 4:35). There are some Consuelos out there where you live. Soul-winning eyes. Could God not do the same for you?

*   *   *

Your Response

Will you make this decision? God helping me, I will endeavor <u>to have a part</u> in winning at least one person to Christ within one year.

If that's your promise, sign here.

_____

Signature

_____

Date

125

Notes

Chapter 1

1. Janet is not her real name. The names of many individuals cited in this book will be changed to protect their privacy. The case histories are true.

2. Michael Green, *Evangelism in the Early Church* (Grand Rapids: William B. Eerdmans Publishing Co., 1970), 48.

3. Ibid., 70; Luke 24:48; Rom. 8:16.

4. Green, *Evangelism,* 72.

5. John 2:22; 3:11, 32-33; 5:32, 36-37, 39; 8:13-14, 18; 9:4; 10:25; 15:26; 16:13; 18:37; 19:24; 1 John 5:10. See Green, *Evangelism,* 75.

6. Charles Shaver, "The Art of Handling Objections/Defending the Faith," in *The Art of Sharing Your Faith,* ed. Joel D. Heck (Tarrytown, N.Y.: Fleming H. Revell Co., 1991), 154.

7. Michael Green, *Matthew for Today* (Dallas: Word Publishing, 1989), 15, 113.

8. Robert Coleman, *Nothing to Do but to Save Souls* (Grand Rapids: Francis Asbury Press, 1970), 53.

9. Quoted ibid., 53-54.

10. Quoted in C. E. Autrey, *The Theology of Evangelism* (Nashville: Broadman Press, 1966), 81.

11. Green, *Evangelism,* 249.

12. The source of this story is Dr. Jesse Middendorf, senior pastor, First Church of the Nazarene, Kansas City. Previously he was pastor of the men in this story.

13. The previous three paragraphs are adapted from the address, "The Challenge to the Seminary: To Send Out Workers into His Harvest," delivered at Nazarene Theological Seminary, Nov. 19, 1985, upon my induction into the Frank and Gladys Cooper Chair of Evangelism. I will draw on this address in several places in this book, but I will not cite the source each time I do so. Excerpts from this address were published in the *Seminary Tower,* Spring 1986, 5-8.

14. R. T. France, *The Gospel According to Matthew* (Grand Rapids: William B. Eerdmans Publishing Co., 1985), 103.

15. William Barclay, *The Gospel of Matthew,* vol. 1 (Philadelphia: Westminster Press, 1975), 78.

16. These facts are from an advertising piece promoting *Tactful Witnessing Guide,* by Michael Mills (Box 401, Grand Rapids, MI 49588), 1990.

17. Richard Peace, *Small Group Evangelism* (Downers Grove, Ill.: InterVarsity Press, 1985), 24.

18. Quoted ibid.

19. Leighton Ford, *The Christian Persuader* (New York: Harper and Row, 1966), 46. The material in this paragraph was adapted from an address titled "A Call to Personal Evangelism," given at the Evangelism Conference, Church of the Nazarene, Kansas City, Feb. 26, 1987. I will draw from this address in several places in this book, but I will not cite the source each time I do so.

20. Wil Spaite, article in *Central California District Advance,* September 1984, 1.

21. This is a slogan of the "Harvest Now" campaign of Evangelism Ministries, Church of the Nazarene, 1991-92. Yet it is a truth that is valid across the years.

22. I do not know the source of this quote. Certain quotations have become a part of lecture notes that I have developed over 20 years. Although I am certain of the accuracy of these quotations, I do not have the original sources. Several other times in this book, I will use other such quotations. I will not footnote them.

Chapter 2

1. Green, *Evangelism,* 243.

2. Ibid., 237.

3. Ibid., 239-40.

4. Quoted in Autrey, *The Theology of Evangelism,* 5.

5. Green, *Matthew for Today,* 140.

6. Ray Matson, message at Nazarene Theological Seminary, Kansas City, Oct. 4, 1985.

7. David Bryant, *With Concerts of Prayer* (Ventura, Calif.: Regal Books, 1984), 75.

8. Richard Foster, lecture at Nazarene Theological Seminary, Kansas City, Nov. 6, 1985.

9. Paul Little, *How to Give Away Your Faith* (Chicago: InterVarsity Press, 1966), 131. This paragraph adapted from Little, 105-31.

10. F. F. Bruce, *The Epistles of John* (Grand Rapids: William B. Eerdmans Publishing Co., 1970), 119.

11. Green, *Evangelism,* 72.

12. Ibid., 149.

13. If you are interested to better understand what it means to be a Spirit-filled Christian, a sanctified Christian, then see the author's *Basic Bible Studies for the Spirit-filled and Sanctified Life* (Kansas City: Beacon Hill Press of Kansas City, 1991), especially geared for individual study or to study with a friend. For a more thorough treatment see the author's *Living in the Power of the Spirit* (Kansas City: Beacon Hill Press of Kansas City, 1986), which is geared for discipleship group study.

14. Green, *Matthew for Today,* 114.

15. See note 13.

16. James Engel and H. Wilbert Norton, *What's Gone Wrong with the Harvest?* (Grand Rapids: Zondervan Publishing House, 1975), 13.

17. Quoted in Dick Eastman, *No Easy Road* (Grand Rapids: Baker Book House, 1971), 58. For those interested in deepening their prayer lives, see the author's *Lord, Teach Us to Pray* (Kansas City: Beacon Hill Press of Kansas City, n.d.), a series of audiotapes based on Jesus' teachings on prayer in Luke 11:1-13.

18. Quoted in Roger Palms, *Enjoying the Closeness of God* (Wheaton, Ill.: Tyndale House Publishers, 1982), 186.

19. See Rosalind Rinker, *Prayer—Conversing with God* (Grand Rapids: Zondervan Books, 1972), for many helpful concepts about prayer.

20. For those interested, the author's testimony is in audiotape form and titled *A New Creature* (Kansas City: Beacon Hill Press of Kansas City, 1988).

21. This paragraph is taken from an article, "The Nazarene Network," *Herald of Holiness,* September 1991, 34. This book's report is a fuller account of those events that appeared in the article.

Chapter 3

1. Barclay, *The Gospel of Matthew,* 1:72-74.

2. Green, *Matthew for Today,* 87.

3. Engel and Norton, *Harvest,* 45. The model included in this chapter is my adaptation of Engel and Norton's model.

4. Shaver, "The Art of Handling Objections," in *The Art of Sharing Your Faith,* 152-53.

5. James Kennedy, *Evangelism Explosion,* 3rd ed. (Wheaton, Ill.: Tyndale House Publishers, 1983), 10-11.

6. William McCumber, *Matthew,* vol. 1, *Beacon Bible Expositions* (Kansas City: Beacon Hill Press of Kansas City, 1975), 70.

7. Barclay, *The Gospel of Matthew,* 1:356-57.

8. Bruce Taylor, message delivered at First Church of the Nazarene, Kansas City, June 5, 1991.

9. A reenactment and dramatization of this call is available in color videotape. It is the author's *Personal Evangelism Call on Mike and Janet* (Kansas City: Beacon Hill Press of Kansas City, n.d.).

10. Quoted in Green, *Evangelism,* 56.

11. Kennedy, *Evangelism Explosion,* 75-76.

12. Dan Durick, "The Master's Chef," *Herald of Holiness,* November 1991, 2 ff. The testimony included in this book is edited from Dan Durick's testimony as he wrote it. The *Herald* version is also edited. There are some differences between them.

13. Win and Charles Arn, *The Master's Plan for Making Disciples* (Pasadena, Calif.: Church Growth Press, 1982), 43.

14. Ibid.

15. Ibid., 63.

16. Adapted from Mills, *Tactful Witnessing Guide.*

Chapter 4

1. Oswald Chambers, *My Utmost for His Highest* (Toronto: McClelland and Stewart, 1935), 165.

2. Peace, *Small Group Evangelism*, 38.

3. Bill Bright, "Personal Evangelism: Conquering the Fear of Failure," in *Evangelism in the Twenty-first Century*, ed. Thom Rainer (Wheaton, Ill.: Harold Shaw Publishers, 1989), 157.

4. Keith Wright, "Dealing with Fear in Personal Evangelism," in Beverly Burgess, *Personal Evangelism Training: Trainee Study Guide* (Kansas City: Beacon Hill Press of Kansas City, 1986), 19-21.

5. Charles Shaver, "The Nazarene Network," *Herald of Holiness*, September 1991, 24 ff., carried this report. I have made some adaptation.

6. I do not say the Christian should never go into these situations. A Christian friend, who is a business executive, is expected to go into social activities where liquor is served. He has done so and maintained a powerful testimony. I myself have gone into similar situations. When we do, we must be careful not to create an impression of compromise. What I am suggesting here is a pattern that will work over a wide range of situations for a wide range of people. Thus, for most people, the guideline "Keep control of the situation" will work best.

7. These last few paragraphs draw heavily on the excellent material in Little, *Give Away Your Faith*, 26-53.

8. J. B. Perry, *A Season Till Spring* (Kansas City: Beacon Hill Press of Kansas City, 1991).

9. Ann Kiemel Anderson, "The Art of Being Human," in *The Art of Sharing Your Faith*, 21.

10. Denny Noland, "I'm Giving My Trade to God," *Decision*, June 1991, 4-5.

11. The Evangelism Ministries of the Church of the Nazarene has a highly rated program of personal evangelism training. You may obtain information about personal evangelism workshops by contacting Evangelism Ministries, Church of the Nazarene, 6401 The Paseo, Kansas City, MO 64131, 816-333-7000. Books that are valuable are Beverly Burgess, *Personal Evangelism Training: Trainee Study Guide*; Beverly Burgess, *Personal Evangelism Training: Leader's Manual* (Kansas City: Beacon Hill Press of Kansas City, 1986); James Kennedy, *Evangelism Explosion*.

12. Robert Coleman, *The Master Plan of Evangelism* (Westwood, N.J.: Fleming H. Revell Co., 1968), 74.

13. Charles Shaver, "The Harvest Is Coming In," *Grow*, Summer 1991, 22.

14. Quoted in Eastman, *No Easy Road*, 58.

15. Gordon MacDonald, *Forging a Real World Faith* (Nashville: Oliver Nelson, 1989), 17.

16. Norman Grubb, *Rees Howells, Intercessor* (Philadelphia: Christian Literature Crusade, 1954).

17. Anderson, "The Art of Being Human," in *The Art of Sharing Your Faith*, 15-30.

18. Gordon Cosby, *Handbook for Mission Groups* (Waco, Tex.: Word, 1975), 10.

Chapter 5

1. Leighton Ford, *The Christian Persuader,* 95.

2. Green, *Evangelism,* 123.

3. For an understanding of the danger of backsliding and the loss of one's salvation, see W. T. Purkiser, *Security: The False and the True* (Kansas City: Beacon Hill Press of Kansas City, 1974). This book is filled with Scripture.

4. Shaver, "The Art of Handling Objections," in *The Art of Sharing Your Faith,* 163.

5. Charles Colson, *Loving God* (Grand Rapids: Zondervan Publishing House, 1983).

6. This illustration is from Charles Shaver, *Living in the Power of the Spirit,* 91. The original source from which the adaptation was made is *Have You Made the Wonderful Discovery of the Spirit-filled Life?* (San Bernardino, Calif.: Campus Crusade for Christ, International, 1966), 2-3. Used by permission.

7. Special help will be obtained both in leading people into entire sanctification and establishing after entire sanctification by use of *Basic Bible Studies for the Spirit-filled and Sanctified Life.* For more detailed training on how to lead people into entire sanctification, see Beverly Burgess, *Personal Evangelism Training II Leader's Manual* (Kansas City: Beacon Hill Press of Kansas City, 1991) and Burgess, *Personal Evangelism Training II Trainer's Study Guide* (1991).

8. This outline was adapted in 1985 from Kennedy's *Evangelism Explosion* by Evangelism Ministries, Church of the Nazarene. The adaptations make biblical and theological improvements over Kennedy. The italicized items have been added by Dr. Shaver as statements he has found helpful in presenting the gospel.

9. William Kelly, "Creed," in *Baker's Dictionary of Theology,* ed. Everett Harrison (Grand Rapids: Baker Book House, 1960), 149.

10. William Abraham, *The Logic of Evangelism* (Grand Rapids: William B. Eerdmans Publishing Co., 1989), 149.

11. Beverly Burgess, *You Can Be a Witnessing Christian* (Kansas City: Beacon Hill Press of Kansas City, 1990), effectively explains four different soul-winning or personal evangelism plans that are in use today.

12. Green, *Evangelism,* 207.

13. Charles Swindoll, *Come Before Winter* (Portland, Oreg.: Multnomah Press, 1985), 43.

14. Ibid. and James Kennedy, *Evangelism Explosion,* 70-76.

15. Green, *Evangelism,* 62-63.

16. "Chic" Shaver, *Personal Evangelism Call* (Kansas City: Nazarene Publishing House, n.d.). This is an audiotape. Charles "Chic" Shaver, *A Personal Evangelism Call on Mike and Janet,* a video. Beverly Burgess, *Personal Evangelism Training Leader's Manual.*

17. Lee Bandy (Knight-Ridder Newspapers), "Atwater: 'I Found Jesus,'" *Kansas City Star,* Nov. 3, 1990, A-4.

Chapter 6

1. Colson, *Loving God,* 92.

2. Green, *Evangelism,* 123.

3. CBS News, June 11, 1991.

4. Floyd Shacklock, *Man of Two Revolutions: The Story of Justo Gonzales,* quoted in Roger Palms, *Closeness of God,* 184.

5. Abraham, *Logic of Evangelism,* 95.

6. Green, *Evangelism,* 61.

7. James McGraw, "Editorial," *Preacher's Magazine,* March 1976, 2.

8. Grant Swank, "Evangelism Must Return to Biblical Basic," *Preacher's Magazine,* March—May 1991, 34.

9. France, *Matthew,* 103.

10. Green, *Matthew,* 130.

11. For more help on commitment, see note 16 in chapter 5.

12. The author's *Basic Bible Studies for New/Growing Christians* (Kansas City: Beacon Hill Press of Kansas City, 1972) is especially geared for adults. For teens, see *Now That I'm a Christian: Basic Bible Studies for Youth* (Kansas City: Beacon Hill Press of Kansas City, 1991). Prepared by Mark Gilroy, adapted from Shaver, *Basic Bible Studies.* For children, see Donna Fillmore and Robert D. Troutman, *Now That I'm a Christian: Basic Bible Studies for Children* (Kansas City: Beacon Hill Press of Kansas City, 1987).

13. Charles "Chic" Shaver, *Conserve the Converts* (Kansas City: Beacon Hill Press of Kansas City, 1976), 10.

14. See previous note. *Conserve the Converts* suggests this one-year discipleship program, p. 68:

> At the completion of the *Basic Bible Studies,* an awards ceremony is held as part of the Sunday service, and the new Christian is presented a diploma to mark his success. This public exposure encourages the convert by the public recognition and puts a reminder to show continued care in the hearts of the congregation.
>
> Many converts ask for another Bible study series after completing *Basic Bible Studies;* and if they don't ask, they probably have the need. An excellent next step is to involve them in a group Bible study. Especially appropriate is the *Beacon Small-Group Bible Studies: The Gospel of John, Part One (Chapters 1—12),* by Charles Shaver. This study should be aimed at continued establishment of the convert and at reaching his unsaved friends. As a young Christian he has friends in the world, but the longer he is a Christian, the more his friends will come from the church. The convert should be urged to invite these unsaved people to a group study while time and circumstances are right. After completion of *John, Part One,* the convert may be urged to do *John, Part Two,* by Shaver. Finally, there is an intensive high commitment study titled *Living in the Power of the Spirit: A Discipleship Study—12 People Meeting for 12 Studies on the Work of the Spirit in the Life of the Believer,* also by Shaver. This will lead believers into the experience of entire sanctification. Together

Basic Bible Studies, the two John studies, and *Living in the Power of the Spirit* make up a one-year discipleship program in manageable segments that all Christians should be led through.

An alternative for *Living in the Power of the Spirit*, if a discipleship group cannot be gathered together, is the author's *Basic Bible Studies for the Spirit-filled and Sanctified Life*. This is used with a spiritual adoptive parent and is eight weeks in length. It also could be used in a small group.

15. Kennedy, *Evangelism Explosion*, 5.

16. Robert Coleman, *They Meet the Master* (Huntingdon Valley, Pa.: Christian Outreach, 1973), 21.

17. Engel and Norton, *Harvest*, 13.

18. William McCumber, lecture at Northeast, Md., Nazarene Camp Meeting, Aug. 1, 1988.

19. Shaver, "The Harvest Is Coming In," 23.

20. Adapted from Charles Shaver, a message preached at First Church of the Nazarene, Kansas City, April 28, 1991.

For further materials on witnessing contact:
Beacon Hill Press of Kansas City
Box 419527
Kansas City, MO 64141

For toll-free ordering phone 1-800-877-0700.